We usually act as if our mental activity is beyond our control; if we are sad or bored, we suffer through it. You can affect your life by mental discipline if you know how. Self-hypnosis is one of the tools that can help you find the sense of well-being and self-gratification that lies within, waiting to be tapped.

THE COMPLETE BOOK OF SELF-HYPNOSIS

John M. Yates, M.D.
and
Elizabeth S. Wallace

IVY BOOKS • NEW YORK

Ivy Books
Published by Ballantine Books
Copyright © 1984 by John M. Yates

Library of Congress Catalog Card Number: 83-17430

ISBN 0-8041-0409-3

This edition published by arrangement with Nelson-Hall Publishers

Printed in Canada

First Ballantine Books Edition: April 1989

15 14 13 12 11 10 9

Contents

Foreword by *Paul M. Balson, M.D.*   vii

Preface   xi

1. Self-Hypnosis: The Basic Facts   1

2. Seven Steps to Self-Hypnosis   16

3. Hypnotic Techniques   29

4. Autoanalysis   48

5. Weight Control   66

6. Living Free of Cigarettes   85

7. Controlling Pain   113

8. Improving Your Sex Life   140

9. Hypnosis Yesterday and Today   154

10. Expanding Your Horizons   173

Index   201

Foreword

Western culture is in the midst of a psychological and cultural revolution of unusual proportions. The former guidelines of nationalism, family, and even religion are being reshaped by the emerging "me" generation. All of us are being asked to gain identity and mastery within the cult of narcissism, where all of life's experiences are focused primarily within the individual and his or her unique perception. We are expected to understand everything we think, feel, and do in terms of its relevance to our own intrapsychic reality and its impact on those people who are important to us. Individual responsibility for productive change and self-growth are paramount, often forcing many of us into periods of frustration or despondency over inner fears of inadequacy in such a competitive and often lonely society.

Individuals such as ourselves, who are caught up in the rush to "inner awareness" and "self-fulfillment," turn to experts for guidance and support. The rapidly evolving individualized experiences (such as Transcendental Meditation), the dynamic and challenging small group experience (such as sensitivity group training or Erhard sensitivity training), and even the questionable massed experiences of the emerging cults point to our unceasing search for adaptational tools during this time of surging cultural transition. We study, read, and imitate others to find a path that matches our capacities with society's demands.

Hypnosis as a self-help technique has a "boom and

bust'' history. Hypnosis has been promoted by the professional and lay person at various times during our culture's history as a panacea for innumerable illnesses or mental struggles. All too often, these unrealistic promises for the power of hypnosis to affect either the mind or the body have led to reactionary periods of disfavor and outright attack of hypnosis as a disreputable technique. Of course, the dramatic distortion of hypnosis as a human experience by the press or the motion picture industry has contributed significantly to its undervaluation or, even worse, its elevation to the ranks of a miracle cure.

The authors of this book have produced a self-help text that portrays hypnosis as a valuable, but not limitless, personal experience and agent for positive behavioral change. Their readable style captures the reader's active attention and participation. As the reader becomes deeply involved with the concepts and techniques of this book (perhaps even ''hypnotically'' involved in the sense of ''experiencing along with the authors''), he or she will almost be able to eavesdrop on the two collaborators working intensely to explore the therapeutic experience of goal-directed self-hypnosis. The reader will intellectually and experientially share the creativity of two people who approached this project from the seemingly quite varied human perspectives of physician and writer.

The authors share their ideas with such intensity and clarity that all readers will be able to accept those concepts and techniques that fit their personalities and reject those that do not. Experiencing students may obtain much from one chapter or the entire text depending on what they choose to accept as reasonable and appropriate in the context of their present and future life circumstances. I urge you as reader to be as daring as you wish in terms of the ideas in this book, but as with all self-hypnosis, stay the ''master'' of your own experiences and wishes in terms of goals and behavior change. ''Read, practice, and apply'' are the words of advice I offer to the reader, keeping in mind Dr. Yates's suggestion that if a particular hypnotic experience or behavioral practice results in success, enjoy that positive change as an indication of your innate hypnotic creativity. However, if careful practice does not result in positive change or results in more emotional discomfort than seems appropriate, the student of self-hypnosis should share such a dilemma with a trained physician or psychologist.

Your learning and practice of self-hypnosis will produce an internalized, active agent for change as long as you maintain the skills. The future contribution of self-hypnosis to your ability to cope with stress or your ability to seize new growth opportunities cannot be predicted. However, continuing practice will enable you to apply it as creatively as possible throughout your life experience.

Paul M. Balson, M.D.
Assistant Clinical Professor
Department of Psychiatry
University of California
San Francisco, and
Chief, Psychosomatic Medicine Services
Letterman Medical Center
San Francisco.

Preface

The Complete Book of Self-Hypnosis takes the wraps off a subject too long shrouded in mystery and magic. A useful guidebook for the beginner as well as a source book for the clinical practitioner, this book lifts the fog to reveal the scientific facts and practical uses of self-hypnosis.

The impetus for writing it springs from a clinical need I noticed in my own practice of clinical psychiatry, a need for reference material to help my patients learn to use self-hypnosis to master their own lives. Currently available books and articles, I felt, were simply not up to what I required. They were either too technical, written in a textbook format, or too much the other way—vague, pollyanna-ish, and impractical for the serious lay student of hypnosis.

My hopes for this book are twofold: (1) to make the process of hypnosis understandable and available to anyone, and (2) to provide practical information about how to use self-hypnosis to take direct charge of one's own life and make positive changes.

A careful attempt has been made to present both the facts of hypnosis and the theory behind it in a clear, concise manner. The goal here was not to overburden the reader with philosophy but to provide an uncluttered, step-by-step approach. For this reason, the whole book and the separate self-help chapters have been organized to present general information, specific techniques, and case histories showing how real people have used hypnosis to make the changes they want.

In essence, *The Complete Book of Self-Hypnosis* is an attempt to represent me when I cannot be there. People themselves are the primary motivating power in hypnosis; the therapist is merely the catalyst. This book is designed to be that catalyst. In it, I have tried to anticipate questions, forestall difficulties, and offer support, help, and guidance.

The help that hypnosis offers the person who wants to make life changes is a personal and individual thing. It is a way to discover how to make your body and mind work *for* you instead of against you. Whatever rewards you reap through hypnosis, the credit will belong to you alone.

In my clinical experience, the results obtained through hypnosis are almost always gratifying. Self-hypnosis is a well-proven way to reinforce positive behavior, mainly because each step offers some form of success. Generally, people's success with hypnosis falls into one of three categories:

1. Instant, dramatic success, where the goal of therapy is reached in one session. This type of response is relatively rare and often the change effected is only temporary.

2. Gradual success, leading to a dramatic point which the person is likely to describe as a "hypnotic breakthrough." This kind of response is the result of a learning process, and the breakthrough is simply a continuation of that real learning.

3. Gradual mastery of hypnotic skills similar to the way a person learns to play a musical instrument or speak a foreign language. This kind of response is often more enduring than the first type, but less dramatic than the second.

The pattern you follow as you learn self-hypnosis will mainly depend on what your personality is like and how much effort you put into the learning process. Like anything else, the more interest and effort you expend, the more rapidly the rewards and payoffs will come.

My own experience with self-hypnosis fell into the second category. When I was sixteen, I injured my neck playing football, an injury that would have resulted in chronic neck pain and a possible drug dependence. I happened to read a paperback book on hypnosis. Skeptical but hurting, I experimented with the induction techniques given in that book and practiced them regularly for about a week. I found them only mildly relaxing until, one night, while concentrating on relaxing my whole body, I accidentally left out the right side in my instructions to myself. I'll never forget the amazement I experienced when I realized the left side of my body was pleasantly numb, the left side of my neck warm and liquidly relaxed, entirely pain free. The right side still hurt, and I felt like a fine line separated one side of my body from the other. On one side of the line there was pain; on the other, freedom from pain.

I've used self-hypnosis almost every day since then for the chronic degenerative arthritis in my neck, and I speak from experience. Self-hypnosis works!

THE
COMPLETE
BOOK OF
SELF-
HYPNOSIS

1. Self-Hypnosis: The Basic Facts

Stepping outside after an absorbing movie, a young couple stands blinking on the sidewalk, gradually readjusting to the world around them.

Bing Crosby's mellow crooning of "White Christmas" pleasantly recalls the Christmas spirit.

While driving home, a woman suddenly becomes aware that she has driven past her turnoff.

A college student's heart begins to hammer as he realizes that the instructor has called on him. He doesn't know the answer. He doesn't even know the question, so lost has he been in a daydream.

These are examples of common hypnotic experiences. Everyone has them almost every day. A hypnotic experience can be defined as an altered state of consciousness, characterized by a sense of inward focusing and temporary inattention to the ordinary environment.

Movies, meaningful songs, the monotony of the

road, and daydreaming are only some of the ways we experience hypnosis daily. Other examples are television, jogging, reading, or any experience which offers temporary escape from routine thought patterns.

Learning self-hypnosis is simply learning to harness and control your mind's natural tendency to retreat occasionally into subconscious reflection. Since you have already experienced various forms of hypnotic reveries, this book can help you enhance your natural talents and use self-hypnosis to its full potential.

Motives for Self-Hypnosis

Why did you buy this book? If you answer that question you will express your own major motive for learning the techniques of self-hypnosis. Perhaps your interest stems from a search for pleasure or a desire to learn more self-control. Maybe you are looking for a way to relieve pain, anxiety, or self-doubt. Or, you could be ready to stop smoking or lose weight. These motives provide legitimate, possible uses for self-hypnosis.

Often, there is a massive neglect of the inborn human capacity to gain satisfaction and a sense of well-being through inner resources. Actually, each person has a fantastic on-board computer so powerful and well equipped that it makes any manmade device, such as drugs or alcohol, insignificant in comparison.

The hardest part of using your mind is getting a handle on its controls, learning which buttons to push on your on-board computer. We usually act as if our mental activity is beyond our control; if we are sad or bored we suffer through it. You can affect your life by mental discipline if you know how. Self-hypnosis is one of the tools that can help you find the sense of well-being and self-gratification that lie within, waiting to be tapped.

It will take patience and dedication to learn the techniques offered in this book, and what you get out of it will depend in part on the effort you put in. Self-hypnosis can help you bring about the changes you want, give you more control over your life, and provide you with a constant resource for pleasure, satisfaction, and feelings of self-worth.

The Hypnotic Trance

The most common misconceptions about the trance state are that it involves unconsciousness, loss of control, and amnesia. On the contrary, most people who achieve trance find it a state of consciousness with "inward focus." While focusing inwardly in hypnosis, one is aware of outside stimuli and can make decisions and act appropriately. In self-hypnosis, you control your thoughts and actions, and that control can affect you in positive ways.

In general, the individual's experience under hypnosis is of three types:

1. Kinesthetic or body feelings. These can involve sensations of floating, lightness or heaviness, sinking, rocking, or swirling motions. Under

hypnosis, many people report a heightened
awareness of bodily sensations.

2. *Visual imagery.* What goes on in your "mind's
eye" during the hypnotic trance can seem as
vivid as real life, often involving reliving of different experiences with all the visual and per-
ceptive sensations that were present at the time
of the experience. Sight, smell, taste, touch, and
hearing are all reported in hypnotic fantasies as
actual perceptions, not simple memories.

3. *Thinking experiences.* "Let me sleep on it" as
a problem-solving technique is similar to what
can be experienced in the hypnotic trance. The
subconscious thinking through that takes place
during sleep can be utilized during hypnosis.
Concentrating on and dealing with problems
through self-hypnosis, one often finds the correct solution at a subconscious level.

Types of Trance

The hypnotic trance is different and unique for each
person who achieves it. What your trance will be like
depends on, among other things, your personality type.
If, when you retreat into everyday hypnotic experiences, you feel relaxed and calm, then that is probably
what self-hypnosis will be like for you. If, however,
you feel hyperacute when studying or concentrating
on, for instance, a tennis match, then you will probably experience a sense of increased awareness when
you reach your hypnotic goals.

The hypnotic trance may be light, medium, or deep.
The barriers separating each are tenuous and flexible,

but the basic characteristics of each level can be described.

Light Trance

People experiencing a light trance are calm and relaxed, aware of bodily inertia, and feel separated from cares, pressures, and demands. For instance, in a light trance, one can lose the social tension that is often a part of human interaction. There may be decreased tension and a pleasant, detached self-assurance with a sense of inner tranquility.

Physically, facial muscles relax, making the face more or less devoid of expression. The overall level of muscular tension decreases, respiratory patterns even out and slow down. The rate of heartbeat and blood pressure usually drop, with the resulting feeling of relaxation. The eyes, if closed, remain closed, although the lids may flicker occasionally, with varying rapid eye movement. If the eyes are open, they are somewhat unfocused and display less visual seeking (looking around the room).

Medium Trance

People experiencing a medium trance sometimes feel disjointed from their bodies, a sensation many times accompanied by changed bodily perceptions (feeling smaller or larger, floating or drifting in space). Concentration is hyperacute, with the ability to turn the senses on or off at will. One may see or not see, hear or not hear. Time perception is altered, thirty minutes may seem like four or five minutes and vice versa. There is a sense of inner-centeredness, comparable to Yoga or Transcendental Meditation. Surgery may be performed without pain on people in a medium trance since they can turn bodily sensations up or down at will.

The physiological characteristics of a medium trance are similar to those of a light trance, but more pronounced. In a medium hypnotic trance, the gag reflex (swallowing) disappears and visible bodily motions slow down or stop, except when accomplishing a hypnotic task or carrying out suggestions. Often, when carrying out a hypnotic task, respiration increases yet the person reports no sense of strain or effort. Involuntary responses to external stimuli may occur, and people in a medium hypnotic trance may open their eyes and talk while maintaining the same level of trance.

Other physiological changes might include spontaneous amnesia or the induction of profound amnesia. Hallucinations may be experienced, both positive (seeing something not there) or negative (not seeing an object in the room). Internal functions may be brought under the person's control. For instance, some people can learn to control their gastrointestinal tract in a medium trance, erasing such symptoms as gas pain, hiccoughs, or heartburn. Age regression is possible at this level (a technique which will be demonstrated in chapter 4). The skin and muscular tone of a person in a medium trance may be very relaxed.

Deep Trance

All the characteristics of light and medium trance may be present in deep trance, with the addition of a blood pressure drop to as low as 50/0. Major surgery may be performed without pain, and positive and negative hallucinations may be induced posthypnotically.

The person in a deep hypnotic trance often has a masklike face, profound muscle relaxation, and a distorted sense of time (expansion or condensation). The profound emotional changes described by people in a deep hypnotic trance resemble nirvana in Yoga or Zen's satori.

This is by no means a complete list of the changes people can experience in the various stages of hypnosis. It is merely an indication of the possibilities that exist. What your trance will be like depends upon your expectations, your dedication to pursuing your hypnotic goals, and your motivation for change. Your experience will be under your control at all times.

Personality Traits That Indicate a Good Hypnotic Subject

There are five major personality traits indicating a good hypnotic subject:

1. *Intelligence.* The best hypnotic subjects are bright, curious, adaptable, and willing to add a new skill to their repertoire of learning experiences.

2. *Motivation.* Simply wanting to learn self-hypnosis is sufficient motivation for successful induction. A desire to effect inner change is also helpful.

3. *Concentration.* A strong indicator of hypnotic success is the ability to concentrate intently, to purposefully focus your energy.

4. *Controlled distractability.* If you can maintain your concentration in the midst of distraction, you are liable to be a good hypnotic subject. For instance, if you can read and comprehend what you read in a room where children are playing or the television set is on, you have controlled distractability.

5. *Cooperation.* Willing cooperation with others and with yourself is often a prerequisite for successful self-hypnosis.

These five general personality traits indicate good hypnotic subjects, but more specific indications include a propensity for daydreaming, doodling, becoming "lost" in listening to music or reading, fantasizing, or pursuing such hypnotic activities as jogging, playing chess, and meditating.

Contraindications for Self-Hypnosis

People who are deeply emotionally troubled or incapacitatingly depressed or anxious should realize that no book is a proper substitute for psychotherapy or other medical treatment. If you feel so depressed that suicidal feelings often surface, or if your life seems unbearable due to anxiety, then you should not use self-hypnosis as an excuse for delaying professional help.

A person with repeated hospitalizations for psychotic or severely neurotic mental states should consult his or her physician before using this technique. It can be a positive help but could also impede needed medical help. Self-hypnosis can be used as an adjunctive treatment for people with such serious problems as alcoholism or drug habituation or addiction, but only if approved by their therapists.

Children, because their reasoning processes are not fully developed, should not be taught self-hypnosis. They should not be hypnotized by their parents, and only a well-qualified psychiatrist or psychologist should use hypnotic therapy with children. Also, self-hypnosis is often not possible for the profoundly mentally retarded and those with organic brain syndromes or other neurological diseases that limit concentrating ability.

If you are going through an emotional crisis such as separation, divorce, or the death of someone close to you, self-hypnosis may not be a good idea. The emotional changes involved may affect your hypnotic experiences and lessen your control. One of the rare untoward hypnotic experiences I have witnessed was a woman who volunteered to be a hypnotic subject for a medical school experiment. She achieved a deep trance and was subsequently awakened and left the auditorium. Half an hour later, the campus police returned her to the auditorium after she was unable to find her car. She was in a state of acute confusion, crying and somewhat disoriented. The hypnotist immediately rehypnotized her and discovered that her divorce had become final that day, and she was undergoing an acute situational reaction. Her particular case was then dealt with both under hypnosis and after she was awakened. This took approximately fifteen minutes. Her confusion and disorientation ceased and she was able to resume her normal activities. This is an example of how strong emotions can affect those under hypnosis.

Although self-hypnosis can be used under the influence of mind-altering drugs, such as marijuana, barbiturates, alcohol, and hypnotic sedatives (Valium, Librium, etc.), as in all things, common sense and moderation should guide the user.

Benefits of Self-Hypnosis

The possible benefits of self-hypnosis are endless and depend mostly on what you want and expect from the experience. Most people report an increased sense of relaxation, self-sufficiency, self-control, self-esteem, and especially a feeling of relief at succeeding in doing something for themselves without dependence on others.

More specifically, clinical evidence supports the beneficial effects of hypnosis on tension, pain control, stopping harmful and unhealthy habits, sexual dysfunction, weight control, psychosomatic illnesses, insomnia, phobias, and many other human problems. These benefits will be discussed at length in subsequent chapters.

Myths of Hypnosis

Myth 1: Hypnosis does not exist. There is a school of thought that believes hypnosis to be a sham state created out of the subject's desire to please the hypnotist. This myth is easily refuted by many documented cases of major surgery performed under hypnosis. Hypnosis does exist, and people do control their pain "under the knife." It is hard to see how something that doesn't exist could be so effective.

Myth 2: Some people can't be hypnotized. Although I can't guarantee this is only a myth, I believe most normal persons can experience hypnosis. Some experiments suggest that people are born with a hypnotic ability which remains at a constant level throughout life. From my experiences in clinical practice, I don't believe that this is true. In fact, people seem to improve with practice and become better hypnotic subjects.

Myth 3: People who can be hypnotized are suggestible, weak, or longing to be dominated. This is the oldest myth relating to hypnosis. Medical textbooks written before the turn of the century described hypnosis as the domination of the weak patient by sheer force of will. Therapists were advised to stare intently at their subject, maintaining a bearing of superiority. By the strength of his character, the therapist was assured control over his weak subject. By standing higher than the patient and using forceful physical gestures to "fix the attention and subjugate and dominate the patient," medical hypnotists attempted to effect healing control over their patients. The myth of the weak, longing-to-be-dominated hypnotic subject has little merit today. As a matter of fact, determined and strong-willed people often make the best hypnotic subjects.

Myth 4: Anyone who can be hypnotized is mentally ill. This is also an old myth, popularized by Jean-Martin Charcot, one of the most eminent neurologists of Europe. He stated over a century ago that the ability to be hypnotized was a diagnostic symptom of a mentally ill person suffering from hysteria. A bitter controversy raged for years until other doctors showed that strong, intelligent, and perfectly healthy people made excellent subjects.

Myth 5: The hypnotic subject must surrender all control. Debunking this is easy when we realize that the subject controls his or her own hypnotic experience in a very definite fashion. In induced hypnosis, the subject merely uses the hypnotist as a pathway to a changed state of consciousness. In self-hypnosis, the subject makes it on his own, using the changed state of consciousness for his or her own purposes. All forms of hypnosis are active, controlled efforts of the subjects themselves.

Myth 6: Hypnosis is a type of sleep, and the subject is unconscious. Studies show that the electroencephalograph (measured brain patterns), or EEG, of a person experiencing hypnosis is similar to the normally alert EEG and does not show the brain-wave patterns of sleep. Many patients report increased alertness during the hypnotic state. In the relaxed state of hypnosis, the subject may appear to be asleep, but his or her ability to talk, move and think, often more clearly than in the normal state, is retained. Hypnosis can be an effective method to combat insomnia and is often used as a way to drift into natural, deep sleep.

Induced Hypnosis and Self-Hypnosis: A Comparison

Both hypnosis induced by another person and self-hypnosis probably reflect the same phenomena. Light, medium, and deep trances can be induced by either method, with the same results. Hypnosis induced by somebody else, particularly a therapist, is often reported to be more intense. The level of trance can be affected by the relationship between the two people, the hypnotist and the subject. There is a natural element of expectation and excitement for both the subject and the therapist, especially if there is a trusting relationship.

When hypnosis is induced for medical reasons, the relationship between the therapist and subject can facilitate and enhance the hypnotic experience. The clinical setting influences a heightened level of trance, with the array of diplomas, stethoscopes, and medical paraphernalia carrying tremendous weight to speed along the hypnotic process. Many of my patients, for instance, are already in a hypnotic state when they enter my office, simply because that place offers many subliminal clues that hypnosis is going to occur. Help is on the way, and a changed state of consciousness is not only possible but expected. Unquestionably, the desire to please the therapist also contributes to the intense level of trance often achieved in medical hypnosis.

Nightclub entertainers who are hypnotists use this theory to induce rapid hypnotic trances in their carefully chosen stage volunteers. The interaction with the audience wages a powerful influence on the subject, and it is a rare person who will wish not to cooperate with the combined pressure of the stage hypnotist's appeal and the expectations of the crowd.

Neophytes to the field of hypnosis can induce trance in each other through these same guidelines. The combined desire to experience hypnosis can be a decisive aid to success. The biggest factors are self-confidence and a willingness to enter the trance state. Learning to induce hypnosis with a friend is analogous to learning any new skill. Sharing information and techniques and experimenting with the best procedures for your own experiences can be used as adjuncts to induction techniques.

In self-hypnosis, the person you want to please is yourself. You are the director of your own game plan, defining your own goals, choosing your own induction and deepening techniques. Your most important tools (motivation and concentration) are always available; you can take advantage of them at any time. Inducing your own hypnotic trance means that you can modify your experience from moment to moment and follow the most interesting lines of departure at your own pace and direction.

In induced hypnosis, there can be a slight conflict when the hypnotist instructs you to imagine yourself gently rocking on a sailboat when your mind wants to visualize a hike in the mountains. This conflict of whom to follow is eliminated in self-hypnosis; you are free to follow whatever is pleasing to you.

While hypnosis carries various magical connotations, it is nothing new to the lives of most people. Everyone has had hypnotic experiences, and can use that remembered occurrence to propel him or her into more disciplined and advanced hypnosis. The motive you have for wanting to learn more about the process is your own, but most people come to self-hypnosis out of a desire to change the unsatisfactory aspects of their lives through inner reflection. The hypnotic trance is a specialized event, with many clinically observed phenomena. Light, medium, and deep trances can be achieved as the subject learns and practices hypnotic skills.

Negative myths to the contrary, the best hypnotic subjects have been proven to be intelligent, motivated, cooperative, and able to concentrate and control distractions. However, hypnosis is contraindicated for some. The benefits of hypnosis, like the motives, depend on your expectations and desires.

2. Seven Steps to Self-Hypnosis

Now that you know a little about self-hypnosis, now that the myths are dispelled and you are in touch with some of the motives that sparked your interest in this new skill, it is time to give you the road map so you can chart your own course. The seven steps to self-hypnosis outlined in this chapter can be viewed as an itinerary, a map with step-by-step directions for an exciting trip through your own mind.

Of course, no magic formula exists that will guarantee immediate success in self-hypnosis. You may achieve trance on your first attempt, or it may take you several sessions or even several weeks to reach that state. How long it will take depends on you, your dedication and commitment to change, your desire to harness the energy of your previous everyday hypnotic experiences and make that energy work for you in new and healthy ways.

You may want to hold off implementing the seven

steps until you have finished reading the entire book, or you may feel inspired to begin immediately. Either way is okay. The important thing is the desire to succeed. These steps were developed after years of clinical experience with patients wanting to learn self-hypnosis. They work. For some they work quickly; for others, more slowly. Don't get discouraged if you don't see the results you want right away. Keep practicing. It will come.

There are two different approaches you can consider in utilizing this chapter. You can read and memorize the steps, then work them out on your own. Or, if it will help you to relax more easily, you can tape your own voice reading the suggestions in steps 3 through 7. A tape recording of your voice, speaking slowly, distinctly, and with appropriate pauses, can enhance your individual techniques and save you the possibility of having to refer to the printed page. This step, however, is not necessary, but some people find it helpful initially.

Step 1: Think It Over

Before beginning, go over in your mind your reasons for wanting to learn self-hypnosis. Ask yourself two questions: Why hypnosis? What do I expect from the experience?

Why hypnosis? Have you had any experience with hypnosis before? Have you seen it done, perhaps on TV or in a nightclub? Do you know someone who has used hypnosis to overcome some habit? Have you seen and wondered about magazine and subway advertisements promising cures through hypnosis? Does the idea of hypnosis intrigue you because of its mysterious connotations?

What do you expect from the experience? Do you hope for a sense of accomplishment at learning a new skill? Do you expect to achieve some personal goal or simply know yourself in a new and deeper way?

Once you have some clear idea about your immediate goals, your motivation and expectations, you are ready to go ahead with step 2.

Step 2: Get Comfortable

This is the set-up step, the preparation for self-hypnosis. You need to arrange a time, choose a place, create an environment, and get your body ready.

Time

Arranging a time to practice self-hypnosis can be surprisingly difficult. You need to be relatively interruption free in order to use your time most advantageously. It's easier to give yourself time when you have planned for it, so pick a time that appeals to you.

People with busy schedules often use bedtime for practice sessions, or weekends, or special times when they know they can count on privacy. Some use coffee breaks. I know one nursing mother who sharpened her hypnotic skills while feeding her baby.

In the beginning, you will need several periods a

day to become adept at hypnotizing yourself. Three times a day, for ten or fifteen minutes a time, is usually good to start with. Practice frequently enough to reward yourself with swift success, which makes it easier for you to continue.

Place

The places people choose for self-hypnosis sessions vary as widely as individual personalities. Some people choose lying horizontally on a bed; others prop themselves up with pillows. A frequently chosen position is in a reclining chair, where the body is supported comfortably at all points. Some people choose to work on their hypnotic skills while taking a walk, but most will find a reclining or semi-reclining posture best at the outset.

Wherever you will feel the most relaxed is the best spot for you. A quiet room, free of distractions and interruptions, is usually most conducive to hypnosis, but if you would feel more relaxed outdoors, that's okay too. The place you choose may be indoors or out, in a bedroom, a workroom, or a patio. Whatever place you decide on, stick to it for the first several sessions. A regular time and a regular place that you associate with the hypnotic experience can help you build your skills quickly.

Environment

Choose your environment to suit your personality. If you are most comfortable with acid rock blaring from the stereo system, then that will heighten your hypnotic experience. If, on the other hand, you prefer classical music played softly, use that. Many people require silence and like to dim the lights to increase their inner focus. Arrange your environment to please you, setting it up so that you reinforce all the relaxation measures you already know and enjoy.

Body-set

I usually recommend that people keep their bodies as limp as possible, in a position that is most relaxing for them. Crossed legs for instance, can cut off circulation, creating an uncomfortable feeling of pressure as your body relaxes deeply. Starting out with your body as relaxed as you can make it will cause whatever technique you choose to be more effective. Some techniques have specific instructions about body-set, but, to begin with, use whatever position is most comfortable for you.

Step 3: Choose a Focal Point

While in your relaxed position, focus on your hands. Gently fold your hands together, allowing the fingers to interlock. Keep your gaze fixed on your hands and notice how your hands look with your fingers intertwined, how the knuckles jut up, and how each fingertip finds a resting place between the knuckles of the opposite hand. Look at how your thumbs cross and examine the texture of your skin, the knuckle lines and the tiny network of lines that form the pattern of your skin.

Commit the sight of your clasped hands to memory, observing every detail. Look carefully at all the aspects of your hands you may never have noticed before. Look at the blood vessels that may be prominent in your hands, and notice how they swell and branch and flow, traversing the area of your hands, sending and returning blood to and from your hands and fingers.

Pay attention to the small, individual marks on your hands and fingers that make them distinctly yours and different from all other hands and fingers. Look at your thumbnails and note every detail about them, their length, smoothness or roughness, any lines or indentations present, how the cuticles look, and the size and shape of the crescents at the base of your nails.

Now look carefully at any jewelry you may be wearing on your wrists or fingers, and notice every detail about the rings, watch, or bracelets you may be wearing. Observe how this jewelry looks next to the tone and texture of your skin.

Finally, let your eyes encompass whatever background your clasped hands are resting on, the fabric of your clothes or whatever part of your body on which your clasped hands are resting.

When all these details are fully registered, go on to step 4.

Step 4: See How It Feels

Notice if your hands and arms are being held tensely, rigidly, or tightly. Allow them to relax while keeping your fingers entwined. Notice how the sensations build in your hands, how you are able to feel the fingers touching each other, able to feel them as they wind around each other, as they touch on both sides, able to feel the position of your thumbs, your fingers, even the position of your wrists. You can feel the skin on your hands where your fingers rest lightly on the opposite hand. You can feel the temperature of your hands, the degree of warmth or coolness in your skin. Notice everything about how your hands feel.

Allow everything that you can notice or feel about the sensation of your fingers being intertwined and your hand position to be registered in your mind. Nothing is more important than to monitor your own experience, to see how this experience grows and builds for you. There are no expectations except to be able to monitor your own experience. You have no goal or set pattern except the one of being able to focus and concentrate, to be able to distract yourself from ordinary intrusions and monitor your experience, allowing yourself to deeply feel every perception in your hands. This is something you can do easily but perhaps have never chosen to do before.

And now as you allow your hands to stay intertwined, your fingers intertwined, your fingers clasped together gently, imagine them, see them in your mind as two pieces of wood, joined together by a master carpenter. If you will, see your fingers as two pieces of wood that have been glued together by a most skillful carpenter, just as a carpenter would fashion a drawer with dovetail joints, with the wood overlapping, using only the best glue. Allow your hands and fingers to become glued together very tightly, planed to the smoothness of a dovetail joint. Allow your natural relaxation to occur as you do this. As you focus and concentrate on one part of your body, the rest of your body can relax deeply, normally, and naturally, with a feeling of ease and accomplishment.

As you continue to focus on your experience, allow relaxation to occur as it automatically does when you focus your energy on a particular point, letting the rest of your body relax deeply and naturally. Turn your hands into tightly glued together pieces of wood smoothly planed together, and continue to monitor this sensation, monitor and notice how your hands feel, how your fingers touch, how they feel where they touch, and how they curve smoothly together. Notice the different perceptions in your hands, as if your hands were glued together by the tightest and strongest glue imaginable by the best carpenter in the world.

Step 5: See How It Changes

Now allow your hands to feel so tightly glued together, so increased in fusion that your hands and fingers are like wood, with a wooden, stiff feeling, with the fingers glued together. The rest of your body relaxes very deeply, ever more deeply. Your eyes may begin to close by now. They may be closed or open.

Notice how the rest of your body feels. See if there is any tension in your shoulders, legs, or back. If there is, let it go. Your only task now is to focus and concentrate on your hands, turning them stiff and wood-like, not unpleasant but very stiff, your fingers glued together tightly, fused together as if joined by the finest master woodworker. Notice how, even if you wished to try to separate your hands, you wouldn't be able to, and the more you tried, the more difficult it would be to separate your fingers and hands. Notice how it would be more and more impossible the harder you tried.

Observe how, even as you do this, you may have thoughts sneaking into your consciousness, which is perfectly okay. You may have thoughts like, Am I really doing this? Am I making these changes occur or am I just going along with the program? Am I merely cooperating and is this just something I am doing consciously, or is this a hypnotic phenomenon? Allow these questions to stay at least subliminally in your mind and see what the answers may be.

But, as of now, the only important thing for you to do is to continue to focus on your fingers and hands and notice how that concentration waxes and wanes, how at times your hands and fingers become stiff and boardlike, glued together so tightly that you could not separate them even if you tried. At times, your concentration decreases naturally, somewhat, and the sensations in your hands and fingers change slightly. Even if you tried, you would not be able to separate your hands and fingers, because you have glued them together so tightly.

If there are any distractions, such as traffic noise, bird songs, or bodily sensations, you may allow them to become less important, more at a distance. You will find that you can turn up distractions, becoming hyperacute to sounds or sensations. Or, turn them down. Let them deepen your relaxation, finding that your thoughts and feelings can work for you instead of against you. If, for instance, two people are having a loud conversation in the next room, you will find that you have control over the way you perceive that distraction.

As your experience continues to change, you will notice that it seems to deepen at times, and, at other times, to lighten. As you continue to master this technique, you can anticipate your level of deepness or lightness and control it more fully. You can deepen your trance state at will, or lighten it to reach the level of relaxation that you want at a particular time.

Step 6: Move the Sensations through Your Body

Again, allow the glued and wooden feeling in your hands and fingers to continue, and compare this to how the rest of your body feels. Allow the rest of your body to become as limp as a dishrag, completely relaxed with no tension. If there is any tension in your shoulders, back, scalp, neck, legs, or feet, allow those parts of your body to simply become totally loose, as loose as your hands and fingers are wooden. Move this sensation of looseness throughout your entire body, as loose as a wet sheet flapping on a line, as loose as a rag doll. Let your body continue to relax. You may notice as you continue to allow your hands and fingers to be wooden and boardlike, that your body seems to be floating, becoming lighter, becoming heavier, sinking into the chair, changing, somehow moving. Whatever your experience is like, it is a personal and individual thing. Allow it to continue. But right now, keep your fingers stiff and boardlike, glued together.

Now, if you are ready, go ahead and give yourself permission to let your fingers and hands turn loose. Let them separate and move apart, your hands and fingers no longer wooden. Allow them to return to their normal state. Allow everything about your hands and fingers to feel as it did before, while keeping extreme relaxation in the rest of your body. As you allow your hands and fingers to separate and return to their previous feeling, let them feel as loose, as completely relaxed as the rest of your body.

Allow this to be a signal for you to go into a deep relaxation, deeper than before, as a reward and as pleasant payment for having begun to learn a potentially very important, healthy, and useful technique, a tool which may be a benefit to you in a healthy way in many, many different types of situations. Allow a feeling of calmness, peace, and satisfaction to occur along with the feeling of looseness and relaxation over the rest of your body, and keep this feeling as a reward for having done very well.

Step 7: Coming Out

Allow these pleasant, relaxing sensations to continue as long as you wish. Whenever you are ready, give yourself permission to become fully alert, awake, oriented, and able to discuss your experience with others or to think it over yourself. Allow yourself to keep some of the relaxation as a reward for having done so well. The next time you do this technique, it will be easier, and each time you do it, your relaxation will deepen. Knowing this, let yourself continue to become fully alert. Whenever you are fully alert and awake, go ahead and notice how the sensations change in your body, everything returning to normal except for a decrease in bodily tension.

You will always return to normal except for the things you specifically wish to change, such as feelings of relaxation or control of pain sensations. Of course, this state of relaxation will take place only when you want it to. Simply clasping your hands or seeing someone else clasp his hands will not automatically trigger a state of hypnosis because you simply will not allow it to. This state is under your control, at your direction, and will take place only when you so desire, at the proper and appropriate place and for the proper and appropriate reasons.

Congratulations on having a relaxing first step! Whether you experienced merely gentle relaxation or a deep hypnotic trance, that level was correct for you at this time. As you continue to practice this technique at least five or six times a day over the next several weeks, you will find increased mastery and enjoyment, and a whole new world of inner concentration building up. You will discover pride in your ability to control and do things that heretofore were out of your control, similar to the pride you have felt before when you have mastered a difficult task.

Once again, it is important to repeat that the hypnotic state will always be under your control and will be used appropriately and under the proper circumstances. It will become easier the more you practice, just as anything else does. So, continue to practice, withholding your judgment on the usefulness of this technique until you have put in at least five to ten practice sessions, each ten to fifteen minutes long.

3. Hypnotic Techniques

Countless techniques and variations of techniques for self-hypnosis exist. Finding the one that works best for you can be as challenging and exciting as mastering any new skill. Be prepared to spend time and energy practicing your new skills and adapting them to your own special needs. In the beginning, you may require a quiet place, free of distractions, to induce hypnosis. But, as you practice, you will be able to hypnotize yourself under almost any conditions.

How to Use This Chapter

The best approach to finding the hypnotic induction technique best suited to your individual requirements is to read through the entire chapter. Then, go back and reread the technique you think might work best for you. Choose one and try it several times, giving yourself ample opportunity to experience what that technique has to offer.

After you have had some success in the method of your first choice, try another one and see how it builds on the first, blending and molding the many different ways you can learn to achieve the hypnotic trance. The endless ways each technique can be varied will challenge your imagination and hone your hypnotic skills, bringing you closer in touch with your subconscious self and letting you enjoy each experience as you learn to relax and know yourself better.

Each of the twelve techniques discussed in this chapter seeks only to give you guidelines. The rest is up to you.

Eye Fixation

Eye fixation is the most common technique, often employed by stage hypnotists and seen regularly in Svengali-type movies. If you have stared hypnotically at the white line down the middle of the road or at a blazing campfire or even at your own television, you have already used eye fixation as a method of hypnosis. This is one of the few hypnotic techniques that has a possible physiological explanation. There is some connection between eye movement and a control center in the brain known as the reticular activating system (RAS), which governs, among other things, one's degree of arousal.

To begin self-hypnosis through eye fixation, pick a spot slightly above eye level, such as a mark on the wall or a corner of the ceiling. The purpose of choosing a spot above eye level is to increase eye strain and induce a sense of heaviness in the eyes.

When you have picked a spot, focus and concentrate on it, allowing your body to relax naturally as you focus, automatically and deeply. Notice how the spot seems to change as you focus and stare. Notice the strain and, perhaps, the dry feeling in your eyes. See how the spot may fade, go out of focus, rotate, and change color. As you continue to stare, notice how your eyes feel dry and heavy, how your lids want to close. Your eyes may feel watery or dry, scratchy or heavy. You may blink more or less than usual, and you may begin to keep your eyes closed for longer intervals of time until your eyes naturally and normally close by themselves.

Allow your body to relax, your shoulders to drop. Your breathing may slow down and become rhythmic and regular. Your internal feelings may change as you relax very deeply, ever more deeply. Let these feelings continue and explore what all the sensations are like for you.

Focusing on a Body Part

This relatively easy method involves cooperation with yourself. In a way, you simply focus on your own biofeedback.

Choose a part of your body to concentrate on, for example, your left hand and arm. Close your eyes and focus on your hand and arm, letting the rest of your body relax as it normally will when you are concentrating intently on one part. Notice the sensations in each fingertip of your left hand in succession and the curve of your fingers. Be aware of your fingernails and how they fit and adapt to the ends of your fingers. You may notice that you can almost feel the bones of your hands as you concentrate if you think about each bone and joint and how it functions.

Focus on all the sensations of your left hand and arm, and notice how they are changing. Perhaps they will feel heavy and numb, light and tingling, warm, or cool. Notice any tension in your hand or wrist and concentrate on relaxing that tension, making your hand feel limp and easy. As you focus on your left hand and arm, you will notice that your whole body has relaxed.

Allow your shoulders to drop and the pleasant numb or tingling feelings in your left hand to travel throughout the left side of your body, up your arm, to the shoulders and neck, down the left torso and leg. The entire left side of your body is relaxed, deeply and effortlessly. Compare the sensations in both sides of your body and then, when you're ready, let the pleasant numb or tingling feeling spread to your right side, too. Notice the waves of relaxation as they sweep over your body. Now go on to explore all these sensations.

Focusing on a Physiological Act

Physiological functions, such as respiration, pulse, and heartbeat, are so automatic we hardly ever think about them. Deep concentration on monitoring your pulse, listening to your heartbeat, or concentrating on your breathing patterns can induce self-hypnosis. The rhythm and movement of these involuntary motions are powerfully hypnotic, and you can channel that energy into the induction of self-hypnosis.

Breathing techniques have been a part of self-hypnosis for centuries, and are used in Yoga, karate, the Lamaze method of natural childbirth, and the common cure for anger, "Take a deep breath and count to ten." Since you are probably already familiar with one or more of those examples, we will use the physiological act of respiration to outline this technique.

To begin induction of self-hypnosis through breathing concentration, close your eyes and relax comfortably in a chair. Allow your body to take five breaths under its own control, without you having to do anything but concentrate. Your body will automatically count and with each exhalation you will relax more.

When you feel the pleasant sense of relaxation pervading your whole body, visualize your lungs. See them in your chest cavity; picture them in your mind as they move the air you breathe in and out, bringing fresh oxygen to your body.

When you are totally relaxed and in tune with your breathing pattern, practice using only the upper lobes in the top one-third of your lungs to breathe, letting the rest of your lungs stay completely relaxed. Notice how your lungs feel as you do this; concentrate on the air as it moves through the airways of your body, in your nose and mouth, down your throat, and into your chest. As you breathe with the upper third of your lungs, allow the lower two-thirds of your lungs and the rest of your body to relax limply.

When you want to and it feels right, practice breathing from only the lower lobes of your lungs, noticing how the air flow in those bottom lobes increases the movement of your diaphragm. As you practice this advanced technique, you may notice how your relaxation increases.

When you are ready, use only the middle third of your lungs for breathing, letting the upper and lower thirds relax. When you have experimented with your breathing patterns and have allowed yourself to relax completely, explore what this feels like both physically and mentally.

Active Fantasy

Before beginning a discussion of the active fantasy method of self-hypnosis, here's a word of warning. Fantasies can be pleasant or frightening, so avoid using any method or technique that might cause a problem. If, for instance, you are afraid of the ocean, avoid the beach fantasy as a way to induce self-hypnosis.

The active fantasies I have used most often, especially when teaching groups about self-hypnosis, involve sailing, skiing, walking on an empty beach, or any fantasy that is pleasant and relaxing. The purpose of active fantasies in self-hypnosis is to give you the opportunity to relive a relaxing, peaceful experience so much so that you can taste the salt air, feel the warm sand, or touch the cool water.

The beach and a crackling campfire are two favorite fantasies, since they conjure up so many warm and comforting images. People like to think about how warm the sand feels on their bodies when they lie in it, the color of the sky as it is reflected in the ocean, the salty breeze, and the wonderful feeling of relaxation and freedom from tension that we associate with a solitary walk on the beach.

If you picture a campfire to induce self-hypnosis, you can concentrate on the dancing flames and the way the flames enhance each color as they spring up in glowing cinders. Remembering the way the fire warms your hands when you stretch them out to the flames, you can relive that experience and feel the same sense of relaxation wherever you happen to be.

Whatever your favorite fantasy is, you can use it to induce hypnosis in yourself. Simply put yourself in that relaxed position you are beginning to know so well and see what fantasy your memory tape will choose to replay for you. Close your eyes and relive an experience that is peaceful and meaningful for you. As you do this, notice the quality of the experience, where you are, your surroundings. No one can know what your experience will be like but you. Allow yourself to begin to relive that experience, that place. Smell the odors, feel the feelings, remember all parts of it. Continue to deepen your experience wherever you are and whatever you are doing. Notice how it changes, how it progresses, and how pleasant it is.

Hand Clasping

Using hand clasping to induce self-hypnosis is one of the most ancient techniques. An example of involuntary muscle control, it takes advantage of the body's natural state of subliminal muscle control. Like the automatic pilot of an airplane, your body can make thousands of minute adjustments and movements without your conscious awareness.

To begin, sit in a comfortable chair with your eyes open or closed and link your fingers. Relax deeply. Turn on the relaxed feeling that is beginning to be automatic as you practice self-hypnosis regularly. As tension leaves your body and waves of relaxation sweep over you, concentrate on keeping your fingers pressed together. Suggest to yourself that your hands are glued together with the strongest industrial glue, and tell yourself that no matter how hard you tried, you could not pull them apart. Think of your clasped hands as the joint of a skillfully fashioned table leg, two pieces of wood joined by a master carpenter and glued together so strongly, so carefully, that they seem like one piece of smoothly planed wood. Even if you used all your strength you could not pull them apart; they are welded together.

As you concentrate on your hands, you will notice how the rest of your body becomes more and more relaxed, more deeply comfortable. You have reached that pleasant state of self-hypnosis where your subconscious mind is open and ready to receive whatever suggestions you wish to make.

Progressive Muscular Relaxation

This therapeutic method of hypnotic induction, also called Jacobsonian relaxation, is one used regularly in hypertension and medical clinics. It involves the progressive relaxation of all the voluntary muscles. By voluntarily decreasing the level of tension in your body and skeletal muscles and the nerves that control them, you will be able to make changes in your conscious level of tension. While changing the level of body tension, you can make concomitant changes in your cardiovascular system, which is, of course, regulated by the nervous system. If you can successfully relax your muscles, perhaps your subconscious will take care of relaxing the rest of you.

One of the social workers in my clinic told me he discovered self-hypnosis on his own through this method. While teaching progressive muscular relaxation to patients suffering from a variety of painful symptoms, he gradually discovered that, in describing how to relax to others, he was learning it himself, inducing self-hypnosis and applying it to his own painful, chronic arthritic condition. He became so skilled at relaxing his muscles that he was able to induce hypnosis by merely closing his eyes for a brief second and saying "click" to himself. The word *click* represented to him the process of progressive muscular relaxation.

There are two variations of this method: (1) simple relaxation, and (2) tense and relax. The first method is begun by sitting comfortably, with your eyes either open or closed. Starting with your toes, concentrate on each toe, and relax them one by one, keeping your attention focused on your toes until they are limp and relaxed. Move up to your instep and ankle, relaxing them in the same way, and then continue to move up your body, one leg at a time, concentrating on each part, moving on to the next only when you have completely relaxed each lower part. When your lower body is tension free, continue on with your hands, progressively relaxing your fingers and wrists, your forearms and elbows, one at a time, to your upper arms. Then relax your abdomen and waist, your chest and shoulders. When your entire trunk is in a state of complete relaxation, concentrate on your neck, releasing any tension that may be there. Then relax your facial muscles and, finally, your head. By this time, you will find your body limp and free of any tightness or tension. By continuing to concentrate on the pleasant sensations of total relaxation, you will successfully induce self-hypnosis.

The second method, tense and relax, employs the same movements, with the additional step of tensing each muscle in turn before you relax it. This can double the good feeling of tension relief, plus underline the contrast between tensed and relaxed muscles.

One person I know, who learned self-hypnosis on her own after reading a few magazine articles, uses this method of induction. She imagines a light switch on each of her major body parts, and she goes through progressive muscular relaxation visualizing herself turning off each of her switches. There are, of course, endless variations to this method—find the one that suits your needs.

Autogenic Training

Autogenic or self-produced training was developed by German scientists and is an authoritarian form of positive reinforcement. Influenced by Eastern thought and philosophy and the contemplative goals of Yoga and other Oriental practices, these scientists tried to adapt Eastern methods to the more Spartan ideals of self-control emphasized in Western culture.

To begin autogenic training, sit upright in a chair with your feet firmly planted on the floor. Keep your hands flat on the chair arms, your spine straight, and your neck and head erect. Close your eyes and begin to give yourself commands. You must pause between commands to allow time for them to work. For instance, you can start by saying, "My arms and hands are heavy (pause), my forehead is cool (pause), and my mind is relaxed and peaceful."

Repeat each command several times with a feeling of power, confidence, and calmness, always pausing between commands to allow them to work.

When you have reached a state of complete relaxation through the positive commands you have given yourself, experiment with some of the variations of autogenic training. For example, suggest to yourself that you feel a warm or exciting color in your chest. Concentrate on that sensation, on identifying the color and how it changes in your chest. Spread that color throughout your body, telling yourself firmly and calmly that it is floating through your body and giving you a new and different, thoroughly pleasant experience.

Pendulum Method

This is the method most universally associated with inducing hypnosis in others, but it can be used as a technique for self-hypnosis as well. Staring at a swinging pendulum is actually a combination of eye fixation and ideomotor movements. (See chapter 5 for a discussion of ideomotor responses.)

To begin self-hypnosis using a pendulum, choose a small object attached to an eight-to-ten-inch-long chain or string. A watch or locket will serve your purpose, as will a ring tied to a thread. Rest your elbow on a firm surface and sit comfortably, the pendulum suspended from your thumb and forefinger. Start it swinging with a light motion so that it drifts gently back and forth. Concentrate deeply on the swinging object, letting your eyes follow it as it goes back and forth, back and forth. The rhythmic repetition of the movement will help your eyes into a pattern of intense concentration on the regular, back and forth movements. As your eyes follow the object carefully, the rest of your body will relax, naturally and effortlessly.

As you concentrate on the motion of the pendulum, your eyes may begin to feel heavy or scratchy and your breathing will slow down and become rhythmic and regular, perhaps adapting itself to the rhythm of the pendulum. Suggest to yourself that as the pendulum swings, your body will become as relaxed as if it were in a hammock on a sunny spring day, swinging back and forth gently in the clean spring air. Each swing of the object will deepen your relaxation. You may gear your thoughts to the rhythm of the pendulum, assigning one word to each arc of the swing: I . . . am . . . deeply . . . relaxed . . . my . . . body . . . is . . . heavy . . . and . . . limp.

The pendulum may stop or continue, it may swing back and forth or in a circular motion. If you wish, you may suggest to yourself that when the pendulum stops, that will be the signal for you to become fully alert again.

Totem Technique

Historically, the symbolism of familiar objects has held a position of importance and power in human lives. The sight of the flag, or the cross, or an ambulance release a mélange of powerful and important feelings. The totem technique of hypnotic induction takes advantage of this natural tendency, using a familiar object as a focus for deep concentration.

To begin, sit in a relaxed posture with a small, familiar object on your lap. You might choose a piece of statuary or a small photograph. Whatever you choose, it should have a shape, texture, and color that is pleasing to you. I keep a carved ebony elephant on my desk for this purpose and have used it often in teaching the skill of self-hypnosis.

With your object held loosely in your hands, sit comfortably and begin to explore both manually and visually your chosen totem. Notice and concentrate on its shape, the smoothness or roughness of it and where its texture changes to give it its unique shape. Notice the variations and subtleties of its colors and how they blend into each other. As you concentrate, your body will relax naturally and without your having to think about it, your tension flowing out of your body as you focus on the object in your lap.

Feel the surface of the object, noticing every aspect and angle, and suggest to yourself that as you concentrate your body will relax more and more. Memorize your chosen object, committing it to memory in its every detail and variation, looking at it from every angle as if you were seeing it for the first time. Allow yourself to reach that state of pleasant, relaxed, tension-free ease that you have begun to learn and enjoy.

Hand Levitation

Hand levitation used to be considered a test of hypnotic trance. If the operator could successfully suggest to the subject that his or her hand was rising on its own, then that person was considered a good hypnotic subject. But, since all hypnotic tests are also forms of induction, hand levitation may be included in the induction category. Relying on involuntary body movements, cooperation, and distractability, it is a useful method for inducing self-hypnosis.

To begin, sit comfortably relaxed in a chair with your eyes closed. Concentrate on relaxing your body, perhaps employing one of the methods already discussed. When you have naturally and effortlessly reached a state of relaxation, suggest to yourself that your right arm and hand are feeling lighter and lighter, as if they are filled with helium. Concentrate on the feeling of having your right hand and arm filled slowly and painlessly with helium, noticing how the feeling of lightness slowly increases, gently tugging your arm up, moving it at your own speed. Without having to use any effort at all, your hand rises higher and higher, floating upward toward your forehead.

When your hand touches your forehead, that may be the signal for you to give yourself permission to relax very deeply indeed, to reach that enjoyable state of trance that will be so important for the changes you may want to make later. The experience of relaxing so deeply that your hand rises on its own to touch your forehead should be very pleasant, a way for you to learn more about yourself and explore some of the ways you can influence your mind and your body.

Key Word or Stimulus

This is an advanced technique that, once you have practiced and learned how to induce self-hypnosis, you can use to speed up the process considerably. The technique of key word or stimulus is simply a shortcut to self-hypnosis, employing a word or thought to turn on the memory tracing that contains the hypnotic experience. This word or thought can serve as a hookup to the brain to recall the whole set of feelings known in previous hypnotic experiences and to induce it once again.

One patient of mine learned to hypnotize herself by imagining a spectacular garden of tulips in every color of the rainbow, starting with purple and moving through blue, green, red, and finally orange. When she explored the tulip garden, stopping to examine and reflect on each color, she induced hypnosis by the time she reached the orange tulips. After weeks of practice, she was able to induce self-hypnosis by simply imagining an orange tulip and, eventually, by only thinking the word *orange*.

Most of the techniques already discussed lend themselves easily to this shortcut. The social worker I described earlier who learned hypnosis through teaching progressive muscular relaxation, used the key word *click* to instantly induce the hypnotic state, since the word triggered the feelings of comfortable relaxation he had taught himself to experience through self-hypnosis. Another common word, one I use myself for rapid induction, is *now*.

The totem technique adapts easily to this shortcut; simply imagine your familiar object and let that stimulus induce self-hypnosis. To use the active fantasy method as a key word or stimulus, associate the entire fantasy with one image, such as a campfire, or a word like *beach*.

It is important to realize that you retain control over the word or stimulus you choose to induce hypnosis in this rapid fashion. As you learn and practice the method, suggest to yourself that the word or stimulus will take effect only if you decide it is appropriate. Another person saying the word *now* or *click* or whatever word or thought you have picked will not automatically put you in a trance. Of course, if you hear your key word or phrase on the radio or TV, it will have no effect and will not induce unwanted hypnosis.

Group Hypnosis

It is an undeniable fact of human nature that people can do some things in groups that are difficult alone. Committee meetings, group encounters, and religious revivals are some positive examples of this statement; lynch mobs and terrorism are some negative examples. Learning self-hypnosis in the company of others can heighten your awareness of yourself and others through the technique of group susceptibility.

There are some people, however, for whom group hypnosis would not be indicated. People who have recently experienced the death of a loved one, a divorce, or any major family trauma should avoid group hypnosis. Psychotics and people with severe neuroses should seek professional therapy and not partake of group hypnosis experiments.

Different ways exist to organize a group for self-hypnosis, as many as there are different kinds of groups. The first course of action should be to get together as a group and thoroughly discuss the common aims and motivations, goals, and hopes. Once everyone is in substantial agreement, choose a spokesperson, perhaps a person with some knowledge of hypnosis and its techniques.

Then the spokesperson might talk to the group members using one of the techniques for inducing self-hypnosis, such as eye fixation or focusing on a body part. One way to enhance the group experience is to have each member hold a pencil suspended in the air between thumb and forefinger; the group is told that when each member has given himself permission to relax completely and enter a state of altered consciousness, the pencil will drop of its own accord to the floor. As each pencil hits the floor, hypnosis will deepen for each member of the group. This subtle reinforcement of the hypnotic techniques can serve to create group cohesiveness and heighten the experience for all.

The spokesperson, should your group choose to have one, should be sure to remove all suggestions put in; and he should remind all members that the hypnotic reactions remain under their own control. If a member of the group should have an unpleasant reaction, the best thing is to stay calm, and gently talk that person back to normal. I recommend that any such group have at least one person with formal training in hypnosis and preferably with training in psychology too.

Group hypnosis can have many benefits for all members, not the least of which is forging a sense of unity and caring in which everyone can share information, techniques, and hypnotic experiences.

The techniques for inducing self-hypnosis are varied and as multi-functional as your own imagination. Finding the one that works best for you can be an exciting exploration of your inner resources. The twelve methods described in this chapter range from the simple to the complex and can be utilized alone or in tandem with other methods.

4. Autoanalysis

More people are seeking psychiatric help than ever before. They come for help in dealing with problems ranging from severe mental illness to a simple desire to improve the quality of their lives. Today's shopper in the mental health market is confronted by a bewildering array of available therapies, running the gamut from primal scream therapy to group encounter sessions to traditional psychoanalytic therapy. EST, Gestalt, nude encounter groups, and rolfing (therapy by massage) are only some of the possibilities presently available.

This jumble of alternatives often makes it difficult for potential clients to pick the best method for them. People sometimes base their choice of therapy on what's easily available or the latest fad rather than making a rational choice influenced by knowledge and personal need.

Since it is beyond the scope of this book to explain

the major types of therapies, we're going to discuss instead a modified system of self-analysis that has been found to work for many people. After all, common sense tells us that there are lots of people doing their own psychotherapy every day. The purpose of this chapter is to help you learn to do yours more efficiently.

A word of warning is appropriate here. Self-analysis is not a panacea for all types of mental distress. If you are suffering from a cold, for instance, self-treatment of aspirin, bed rest, and fruit juice is in order. But, if your cold turns to pneumonia, you should hie yourself to your local physician and let him or her help you out. Just as grapefruit juice alone won't cure your pneumonia as penicillin will, so self-analysis may not be enough if you are severely depressed or extremely anxious.

Understanding Your Personality

When a baby is born, two factors are at work to mold it: the unconscious mind (a blend of genetics and the drive for satisfaction) and the environment. The merger of the unconscious and the environment can never be complete. The child learns early, for instance, that milk (environment) isn't always there exactly when it is wanted (unconscious). The conflict that is the result of this dilemma can be felt by the baby as anxiety.

The baby's first cry is the beginning of the road to adult anxiety, the first frustrated signal that needs haven't been met. Even the best parents can't meet all the needs of the infant, nor would it be healthy to do so.

The first way a child learns to deal with this dichotomy, this inability to merge its unconscious with its environment, is repression. He or she learns to repress needs and desires. Parents know this and will help the child to learn to repress by offering the distraction of something pleasant after an unpleasant experience. Lollipops are offered as consolation for bumped heads, and parents hug and fondle a hungry baby until it can be fed.

Inevitably, we learn this technique of easy repression and use it ourselves to put unpleasant things out of our minds. We all have a generalized amnesia for childhood traumas and show an amazing lack of knowledge about our inner self.

Repression is only one of many devices a child learns, such as substitution (accepting a hug in lieu of milk) or displacement (fearing monsters after overhearing a parental squabble). These are important steps in child development. The formation of this brain machinery to deal with conflict is called by psychiatrists the ego structure. (Lay people often use ego to mean a sense of self-love and pride, but we are not using the term this way. For our purposes, ego will simply mean the ways people learn to deal with their surroundings.)

So the formation of the ego as a way to work through conflict allows the child to set up a Compromise Formation, which can be viewed as a personality trait. People learn to be stingy or open, they learn to be controlling or spontaneous, verbose or taciturn. In a thousand different ways the personality forms, leading to a partial resolution of the original conflict. The sum of these experiences is what we call "personality."

It is amazing how angry people become upon being told that they are not always aware of why they do things. People need to feel that they are the masters of their own minds, and it can be disheartening for anyone to realize that much of the motives for their thoughts and actions are rooted in the experiences they confronted in that crucial first year of life. The anger that people feel at hearing they aren't always aware of why they act and think the way they do is the process of denial in action. Many people simply deny they have any unconscious motivations at all!

Freud observed that the pride of humankind has suffered three grievous insults since the sixteenth century. First, Copernicus showed that the earth is not the center of the universe. Then, Darwin's theory of evolution indicated that we are not a special creation, and finally, Freud demonstrated that we are not even the masters of our own minds.

The personality, then, is a summation of the partial resolutions to all the major conflicts. Your personality is a result of the way your ego's defense mechanisms get you through the day. For instance, if you had significant conflicts around separating from your mothering figure and these were only partially resolved, then you may semiautomatically go through a series of behaviors every time you are faced with even a mild or symbolic abandonment. If you see your lover with another person, you may eat a whole bag of chocolate chip cookies (substitution) or you may have four different dates with four different people during the next week (sublimation). You may spend a lot of time crying and feeling miserable (turning anger against self, interjected anger), or you may decide to hate all members of the opposite sex forever (reaction formation). It is especially difficult to see these things in yourself because of the automatic denial mechanism you have built up over the years.

Whatever your personality, you can be sure that your ways of reacting to life in general and crises in particular are adult versions of the methods you learned in early childhood that worked for you. The technique of self-analysis through self-hypnosis can help you uncover some of these significant events and feelings. In learning more about how and why you act as you do, you may be able to bring some of your ways of re-acting (Compromise Formations) under your conscious control.

General Personality Traits

There are many personality types and combinations of types, but for clarification and understanding, this discussion will be limited to four of the most general.

Obsessive

Some people respond to stress by seeking to be more in control of the situation; they develop behavior aimed at maximizing stability and solving problems. The obsessive-compulsive person uses logic and intellectual means and often reports having very few feelings or emotions. It is almost as if their feelings are shut off, denied because they are too painful. This is a defense mechanism that works well for all of us. But, if you carry it to extremes, you may find that your life is empty and dull and you envy others their spontaneity and warm relationships.

The homemaker who "takes care" of her family by cleaning the house all day long, making sure everyone is dressed and fed exactly right, yet feels something is missing in her marriage is a good example of an obsessive personality. So is the man who can never unbend or relax, who wears a suit and tie to the zoo on Sunday and keeps a rigid time schedule of how long the family can view each exhibit.

Hysterical

If you find yourself overstressed by feelings of rejection, if you are constantly searching for appreciation from others or a sense of personal well-being through others, you may be responding to an earlier conflict centered around the need for love. People who have been given only conditional love or from whom love has been too often withheld, fit into the category that is pejoratively termed "hysterical." It was Freud who disproved the popular conception that only women have hysterical personalities by documenting a case of male hysteria. The word *hysteria* derives from the Greek word for uterus.

A better term for this personality type might be "love-seeking," because these people seem to spend most of their time in a search for appreciation and someone to take care of them.

I have seen people whose main source of appreciation seemed to be a relationship with their doctors, who have undergone dozens of operations with a feeling akin to glee. These people come to a doctor seeking relief for a symptom which never seems to be found in surgery. Unfortunately, when diagnosis after diagnosis proves futile, doctors become frustrated and reject the patient by referring him or her to someone else. Often the patient at this time shows an increase in symptoms and anxiety. This rejection is so painful because it symbolizes earlier deprivation of love, and the frantic search for the "right" doctor continues.

If you find yourself seeing patterns which are appreciation-seeking from "strong and powerful" others and a willingness to do almost anything to please, then perhaps you show some hysterical personality traits.

These traits are not all negative, however, and they bring us much of the spontaneity and joy of life. A man and a woman cannot have a spontaneous sex life without some hysterical qualities in both, for instance. Too, the finest actors display many of these hysterical qualities, and, of course, good parents must have some hysterical traits to love their children and to show it.

Depressed

If you find patterns of sadness in your exploration of your interpersonal relations of the past, this may give you a clue to other types of deprivation. The hysterical person seems to be still seeking an almost parental acceptance, while the chronically sad person seems to have given up hope of ever getting this acceptance.

People whose personality type is chronically sad often blame themselves in an unrealistic way and consider themselves unspeakably evil and worthless. If the patterns that show up in your self-analysis are consistently sad or show a sense of loss that cannot be redeemed, and if you find yourself behaving as if things were hopeless and you are helpless to change them, then perhaps you have suffered this quality of loss. It is common sense as well as a scientific fact that an extremely high percent of chronically depressed people have suffered the death of one or both parents before the age of sixteen.

Angry

If your past patterns reveal a consistent feeling of anger, if there is a sense of struggle in your interpersonal relations of the past and present, and if your present behavior patterns fall under the rubric of revolt, then perhaps you have learned to respond to conflict by keeping your anger turned outward.

This is an often-found theme in literature—humankind's struggle against a hostile universe. A little child is often trying to cope with a hostile universe in his or her own home. If this is carried over to adulthood, life becomes a constant battle against an unfriendly world. If you find yourself constantly "telling them off" or symbolically "thumbing your nose" at people, then you may learn more about your angry frustration as you continue your self-analysis through self-hypnosis.

How to Begin

Since it is difficult to really know yourself when your automatic censoring device is working overtime to help you repress what is painful, you will need some kind of structure to help you begin self-analysis. Robert Burns put it as well as anyone in his poem "To a Louse" when he wrote, "Oh wad some power the giftie gie us/ To see oursels as others see us!" ("Oh, would some power the gift could give us/ To see ourselves as others see us").

Step 1: Use some relaxation and tension relief techniques to help yourself set the stage for your first autoanalytic session. Follow steps 1 through 6 outlined in chapter 2, and when you are feeling sufficiently relaxed, go on to step 2 following.

Step 2: Let the question, What sort of person am I? float into your mind. You will get an answer that may be surprising, even to you.

Step 3: When you have your answer, think about the ways you interact with other people. Think about your interactions today with others, and view it as if you were watching it from the outside. Take your time at this and see what you think of yourself. See where this leads you.

Step 4: It is impossible to know what pathways you will follow, but when you have followed the path for a while, return to analyzing your associations with others. This time, see yourself in an interaction of the

past. Allow this interaction to float to your consciousness and once again observe your behavior. Where are
you? What are you doing? What are you thinking or
saying? And, especially, how do you feel?

Step 5: When you feel you have explored the significant interaction of the past, do the same thing with
several different occasions in the past, at any age. Notice everything about the situation and see if you can
feel what you were feeling then.

These steps will be used in subsequent sections of
this chapter.

Emerging Patterns I

After you have followed steps 1 through 5 for a period of time, either one hypnotic session or thirty, a
pattern will begin to emerge. This is what psychiatrists
do—psychiatrists who are psychoanalytically inclined
spend their time waiting for (and helping) patterns to
emerge.

Often the psychiatrist is a subject of humor, who
stereotypically sits in a chair with clasped hands mur-
muring "um-hum," and "How do you feel about
that?" If the psychiatrist is good, however, he or she
constantly evaluates the patterns that emerge in the
patient's behavior and speech. As new patterns show
up and old patterns recur, there is a temptation to describe and to explain them to the patient, but this must
be done at the right time. If it's done too soon, the

patient's automatic denial system keeps him from noticing. The psychiatrist must aid and await the time when the person's feelings and remembrances result in an ''ah-hah!'' understanding. At that point, the patient can recognize his or her own behavior patterns in a new and deeper way and learn that these behavior patterns can be affected.

Through self-hypnosis, you can bypass the couch and monitor your own emerging patterns, gaining insight into yourself and your behavior as you go. Training yourself to notice the patterns that show up consistently as you examine past events and feelings takes practice, but it can be accomplished as you continue your self-analysis through self-hypnosis.

Age Regression

Now that you are beginning to see what themes of behavior run through your life, you may want to explore how they came about as a way to begin to change some of the aspects of your personality presently causing you distress. One way to do that is through the technique of age regression. A medium to deep trance is required, but it can be accomplished through practice and dedication. Follow steps 1 through 6 outlined in chapter 2, and, when you have succeeded in relaxing as deeply as possible, imagine yourself at age ten.

Put your age-ten self on a stage and sit back and observe what that child does, how he or she reacts to whatever significant event is occurring. Let every impression of yourself at age ten sink into your consciousness. What are you wearing? What expression is on your face? Who else is interacting with you? What kinds of body movements do you display and how do those movements reflect your age-ten feelings? Concentrate on your feelings, and try to make the jump from what you felt at ten to how you have learned to cope with those feelings now.

Whatever your experience is like, you may find it strangely disturbing. This is okay. It means that you may be uncovering some important information about yourself and your feelings. You may be beginning to overcome that automatic repression which keeps you unaware of your unconscious.

When you have observed all you can about your age-ten self, close the curtains of the stage you were seeing yourself on and reopen them to see yourself at the age of six. Repeat the process you used to explore at age ten. See what is going on, who you are with, what is going to happen. Repeat this process for ages four and two.

What you are doing is waiting for patterns to emerge. Are you consistently sad or angry? What do you think about that little child you see, that little child who grew up to be you?

You may want to use age regression as a regular part of your autoanalytic hypnotic sessions. The more often you can see yourself clearly in childhood, the more patterns you will begin to see emerging. Each time you use age regression to learn more about yourself, you will make a small inroad into understanding those past feelings and emotions, those past situations that helped make you what you are today.

Dream Interpretation

You may also use your dreams to get hints about your personality structure. Dream interpretation is a common psychoanalytic technique that can be applied to self-analysis through self-hypnosis. The first thing to do to learn how your dreams reveal the workings of your unconscious is to remember them. This can be easily accomplished through self-hypnosis. At night, before going to sleep, use self-hypnosis and suggest to yourself that you will dream and you will remember what you dream. When you wake up, immediately write down everything you can remember about the dream. Keep paper and pencil by the bed for this purpose.

In your autoanalytic sessions, consider your dreams, always keeping an open and questioning mind; look for patterns of dream behavior or feelings that will help you be your own psychiatrist. Whatever patterns you find, you will probably notice that your present behavior is a repetition of past patterns.

Dreams are difficult to interpret because they are often much disguised by your waking censor, your ego. So, don't be frustrated if, at times, you are completely unable to make any sense at all of your dreams. You will notice as you go through this process of monitoring your behavior patterns that you will find many hindrances along the way. After all, your personality doesn't change easily and your unconscious feelings and thoughts resist exposure. This resistance can be seen as healthy because it would be a strange world indeed if our personalities changed from day to day.

Even though dreams often seem bizarre and surreal, through self-hypnosis you may decipher the clues they give you about your personality.

Emerging Patterns II

If you are seriously attempting self-analysis, you already know about the resistances your unconscious can throw up in your way. The value of a good psychotherapist is his or her ability to help you overcome your resistances by helping you notice them and work through them in therapy.

But you can accomplish the same goals and reap the same rewards without the guiding hand of a psychotherapist, if that is what you wish to do. You have already observed repetitious patterns in your past and present behavior and feelings, and now you may be wondering how to use this uncovered information to effect desired changes. Many people realize through self-analysis that simply discovering these repetitious and usually inefficient behavior patterns in a new and deeper way somehow gives them the ability to change them by direct and conscious effort.

Two behavior patterns that often emerge through self-analysis are feelings of weakness and feelings of anger. For instance, if you find it hard to stand up for yourself in all kinds of different situations—with your boss, your friends, or your mate—or if you constantly feel ill-used by the people you love because you find it hard to say no, then feelings of weakness are probably part of your emerging behavior patterns.

If, on the other hand, self-examination reveals patterns of rage, if you have a chronic image of yourself as a simmering pot about to boil over, if a minor social snub colors your whole day and makes you snap at everyone around you, then you know that one of your emerging behavior patterns is that of anger. If you recognize these patterns as counterproductive parts of your personality, parts you would like to change or at least control, then self-hypnosis can be a powerful tool toward that goal.

First of all, you will want to examine those patterns thoroughly and try to determine where they come from. The answer to that usually lies in childhood. You are given a life sentence when you are born: to be like your parents. But that sentence can be commuted. Your internal attorney (your adult mind) can renegotiate the terms of your imprisonment.

Understanding where those uncomfortable feelings come from is crucial to changing them. Now, with your adult mind, you can discriminate among the accumulated patterns of your personality, discarding what hurts you and keeping what is useful. Knowing the enemy—the unuseful patterns that keep getting you into painful situations—gives you an important starting point for change.

How Can You Discard Painful Patterns?

A good way to begin is to put yourself in front of a mirror and, using a hypnotic technique that works for you, put yourself in a trance. You may want to focus on a body part or use your own eyes as the focal point, staring into your eyes until you feel the by-now familiar feeling of relaxation and heightened concentration. Allow yourself to focus on the whole image in the mirror. See what you look like and how you feel about the person in the mirror. Notice how strangely moving it is to look at yourself in this way.

Observe what expression comes to your face as you concentrate. Do you wish your expressions were different? That you were different? Let some new expressions cross your face and see what they are like. Don't force anything; it will come. Let them happen and observe them carefully.

Next, see what thoughts come to your mind. Allow them to happen naturally and effortlessly. What mental images are forming, and what memories hook up with those images? What associations come to mind as you look at yourself? How do other people—your parents, your friends—see you? How does this tie in with your overall patterns? Do you see any connections between what you were told, what you learned to think about yourself in childhood, and what you feel now?

How is your past training and experience affecting your present self-concept? If you were consistently told you were a nasty brat between the ages of one and eight, then somewhere inside that mirror you are going to find a nasty brat feeling.

An interesting deepening technique that correlates well with mirror confrontation is to put yourself in the hypnotic trance and then say your own name aloud. Say it in a normal voice, with no special inflection. This experience, like looking at yourself, will invariably bring out deeper feelings about yourself in a revealing way. In the changed state of consciousness your feelings and attitudes, both positive and negative, can become known. Whatever they are, they will be powerful and personal.

The feelings that come out when you look at yourself or say your name aloud are evidence of how well we learn to repress our deepest thoughts. Repression itself is not always bad, however. We already know it is our major way of dealing with conflict. But now we can also recognize how useful it might be to let some of that repression decrease. This way you can free yourself of some of the Compromise Formations you made long ago that, now you are adult, are no longer appropriate.

As you continue to practice and utilize this technique, you can give yourself posthypnotic suggestions to trust yourself more, have more faith in your inherent goodness. If weak patterns are what you want to change, you can tell yourself, "I may feel weak, and I felt that way as a child, but those qualities are not really a part of me now. I am strong now." If it is anger that has caused you problems in the past, say to yourself, "Sure I feel mad. Now I know why. I choose not to feel that way all the time."

People who use this psychiatric self-help technique will find themselves using it over and over to work through conflicts in their present life, each time getting an enhanced feeling of mastery and self-appreciation, much like patients do in formal psychotherapy.

Conclusion

If, in the course of your self-analytic sessions, you discover alarming or frightening things about yourself, and your self-analysis produces more anxiety than it alleviates, lasting for weeks or months, this is a signal that you may need more structured help. Contact a therapist and get the help you need.

But, if you are like most people, constructive self-analysis under hypnosis can unlock many of the clues that will help you understand why you became the person you are. Whatever knowledge of yourself you gain will admittedly be partial, but it will give you the information you need to bring about important psychological changes, changes you yourself want to make.

Don't engage in an orgy of blame-finding when you discover what happened in the past. Try instead to see how you are still reacting to those events, and then decide what you want to do to change things now. Through autoanalysis you can identify and begin to overcome your resistances and, in the process, give yourself the freedom and permission to make a new friend: yourself.

5. Weight Control

One major cause for obesity is that people eat more than their bodies require. Obesity is a primary American health problem. If you have this problem, this chapter will help you individualize your weight reduction program, using hypnosis as a tool to make it easier.

Medical diagnosis divides obesity into two categories: exogenous and endogenous. Obesity that is exogenous (coming from outside) results from overeating. Common sense as well as medical opinion tells us that a fat person takes in more calories than he or she needs. Lots of people are told by their doctors that they eat too much, and most of them reply vehemently that they don't. I've had lots of patients tell me that they "really don't eat all that much," even though they weigh from 200 to 600 pounds. Once again, we see denial in action.

Doctors are often frustrated and patients are often

angry after a weight-counselling session when the patient claims he or she eats no more than "average." Diets are prescribed and usually not followed, and still the patient insists that food is not the problem. The physiological condition of obesity is almost always the direct result of overeating.

Obesity that is endogenous (coming from inside) is caused by a defect in a person's metabolism, the way the body chemically processes food. This is a rare condition. Doctors like to find a biochemical cause they can treat, so they usually test this category first. Low thyroid function or other hormonal abnormalities can contribute to obesity. Cushing Syndrome, an excess of steroid hormones, is another cause. Steroids in general (hormone shots or pills often prescribed for inflammations, pain, degenerative joint diseases, and many other conditions), if taken over a period of time, have the side effect of obesity. Hypothalamic brain lesions, anterior pituitary deficiency, and gonadal deficiencies are some extremely rare metabolic causes for obesity. But probably less than one in one thousand cases of obesity has a biochemical cause.

Many psychologists describe obesity in terms of environmental and cultural patterns. In some families, life centers around the preparation and consumption of food. Social psychologists see eating behavior as learned and obesity as simply the continuation of an early learned behavior. Just as a child who grows up with violence often becomes a violent adult, so a child who grows up in a food-centered family will tend to be food-centered as an adult.

Sociologists also mention junk food addiction as another cultural pressure toward obesity. The popularity of fast food outlets and preprepared meals assures that a lot of Americans receive more calories and less nutrition than they need.

Some psychiatrists and psychologists are prone to see obesity as a symptom of underlying psychological problems. Many obese patients describe a troubled home environment in those important first two years of life, troubles that revolve mainly around the incorporation of love and food. These patients spend their lives resolving that early conflict by literally eating it. People generally don't like to be told this, as it seems to be an insult.

One patient I know who weighed over 300 pounds said, "I never deny myself anything." His whole life revolved around food. On his regular visits to his mother, he brought huge amounts of food for her to ritually prepare for him. His appearance was like that of a baby, even though he was the successful owner of a string of movie theaters. All his social activities centered around food, and he made sure any need he had would be instantly gratified.

Although this is an extreme example, it illustrates the point that need-gratification is often an important reason for obesity. After all, when we are sad, we speak of a "feeling of emptiness," or describe ourselves as "a hollow shell" or "hungry for affection." When we are happy, we see ourselves as "full of life," "satiated with pleasure," or "filled with joy."

Food can be a reward, and we learn from our earliest childhood experiences that when we have been good, we get goodies. Even our childhood myths are food-oriented: the Easter Bunny brings chocolate eggs, Hansel and Gretel are lured to the witch's candy house, and the annual Halloween trick-or-treat candy feast are some examples.

Overeating can also be an expression of anger. We speak of "attacking a steak," "swallowing" our fury, and what we don't like often gets "stuck in our craw." "Getting a bellyful" may mean getting a bellyful of food or anger.

A patient I once treated came in with symptoms that included not being able to enter a supermarket, experiencing actual nausea if he had to shop for food. As we worked on his problems, we discovered that his father had been an extremely angry and controlling man who chose suppertime to upbraid the children for misdemeanors of the day. This patient felt that he had "swallowed" his anger all his life, and expressed rage that he had not been allowed to play sports as a child because he was forced to work in his father's grocery store after school. With treatment, he was able to control both his weight and his supermarket phobia.

Another reason for obesity can be a defense against close personal contact. Fat people are seldom objects for seduction, and I have seen many people whose "weight problem" was a way of putting distance between themselves and others. One anesthesiologist I treated had never had a date in her life and frankly stated that if she were slender she might have to face up to the fact that she might not be attractive to men.

Sexual attractiveness can seem more dangerous to some people than physical assault. I often feel that some people have built an envelope of adipose tissue (fat) around themselves which protects them in many ways from the risks of seeking mates and love objects. They seem to say to themselves, "Nobody could want to date a fat person like me; if I only lost weight everything would be okay." But they never lose weight and thus avoid the mating game and its attendant risks.

Even though we have been talking about the negative aspects of eating behavior, it's important to remember that food can often be usefully used to express or enhance feelings of love, sex, anger, or reward. It is when a person uses food as an exclusive substitute for one or all of those things that he or she often runs into obesity problems.

Self-Analysis

How you feel about your body will probably be reflected in what you do about it. Some people who go through therapy adjust their body weight accordingly. As they feel better about themselves, they lose weight. People choose their body weight as a reflection of their self-image.

You have already learned how to use self-hypnosis in autoanalysis. Now you can go on and examine specifically why you have a problem with your weight.

The decision to lose weight is the first and most important step toward reaching your goal. You can check out the decision with your unconscious by using the technique of ideomotor movements. To do this, sit in a comfortable place with your hands resting on a flat surface, your thighs, for instance, or the arms of a chair.

Make your right index finger represent "yes" and your left index finger "no." Your right thumb will represent "I don't know" and your left thumb will be "I don't wish to answer."

Using the technique of focusing on a body part, enter a hypnotic trance. Deepen it by counting down slowly from ten to zero, becoming more relaxed with each number. You are going to be asking your unconscious some questions about your desire to lose weight.

First, take a trial run, and ask yourself if you were born on your birthdate. Wait for an answer. Concentrate on your right index finger and notice when it moves without your having to do anything. (If it doesn't move in two or three minutes, give it a little voluntary help, but sooner or later it will move on its own.) Ask yourself some other patently true questions and some false ones to gain confidence in the ability of your fingers to move in response to your subconscious.

Now you are ready to ask yourself the "Big Question": Am I satisfied with my present body shape? Wait for an answer. Concentrate on your hands but do not try to move your finger. It will happen. When your answer comes, it is your signal not to try to lose weight but to do it.

Anything but a positive answer gives you some added insight into your ambivalence about losing weight. If you consciously do want to change your body image, go ahead with the program and continue to use self-analysis to understand more about your feelings about your body weight.

By using what you learned about yourself in chapter 4 on self-analysis, take some time now to see how that relates to your body image and your eating habits. Under self-hypnosis, ask yourself about your body image. Do you see yourself as a fat, jolly man? A pleasingly plump woman? Or do you see your extra pounds as grotesque and disgusting? Most people fall somewhere in between, so follow the steps below and see what you discover.

With your eyes closed, make a movie screen appear on the back of your eyelids and wait until an image of yourself comes onto the screen. See what you look like. See yourself in clothes, in a bathing suit, and without anything on at all. Study those images. Concentrate on them, noticing what your face looks like, your upper body, your stomach and hips, your legs and feet. As you continue to gaze at these images, once again searching for patterns, see if there is any hookup between how you look and what you have learned about yourself to date. Notice that it may take some effort to sustain your concentration since you are not used to self-exploration at this level of concentration.

In front of a full-length mirror and in private, look at yourself with your clothes on, in your underwear, and nude. Then repeat this experience under self-hypnosis. Ask yourself how you feel about those images. Are they right for you? This step is important, so give it plenty of time. At this point, you may decide that you really don't want to lose weight, that your body image is okay as it is.

Under self-hypnosis, ask yourself what has happened in your recent past to make you want to lose weight. Go over the events of your recent past to find out if your desire to lose weight is based on a gradual realization that you want to change your body image. Is it based on a desperate need to improve your health? Are you being coerced by outside forces to lose weight? Are your mate, your friends, your doctor urging you to shed unnecessary or unattractive pounds? Whatever your reasons, your goal is now possible. But, it must be emphasized, only if it is your goal.

Consider your eating habits. When do you eat the most? Do you have regular meals or snack all day? What is your favorite food? Is the anticipation of food more enjoyable than the food itself? Some people don't really taste food beyond the first few bites but keep eating anyway, much like a compulsive gambler who can't stop a destructive habit. Is this true for you? Do you hide food? See how these patterns tie in with others you have already discovered about yourself. Are you a binge eater? Do you eat large quantities well beyond your satiation point? Do you enjoy eating alone or with others?

Techniques

The answers to all the questions you have asked yourself in your self-analytic sessions will help you understand why your eating patterns have made you overweight. Understanding why your body doesn't reflect yourself as you want to be will give you added incentive to change.

Now you are ready to begin losing weight. After checking with your doctor to make sure it is medically okay for you, pick out a good diet which allows you at least one thousand calories a day. You can choose a strict diet plan or simply reduce your caloric intake to what you know will keep you healthy while you lose those unwanted pounds.

Now that you have made the decision to lose weight and checked it out with yourself, believe it or not, self-hypnosis can make the process an exciting adventure. Here are some techniques to make it so.

Enter a hypnotic state shortly before mealtime and eat in a hypnotic trance. Once you start eating, make each morsel as enjoyable as the first taste. Concentrate on the sensation of each bite in your mouth and slow down your eating. Rather than gulp, sharpen and increase your sense of taste with each bite you take. You may choose to change your perception of time as you eat, making each meal a banquet. You will find that food assumes a new and different taste, texture, and fragrance all through the meal. Since you are giving up quantity, you will begin to enjoy quality instead.

If you have discovered that you eat out of a sense of anxiety, using food as a tranquilizer, then use self-hypnosis to calm that anxiety. Whenever you feel the urge to raid the refrigerator or stop at a fast-food joint, immediately induce a hypnotic trance and let the familiar feelings of peace and relaxation calm your anxieties and tame your appetite. Use self-hypnosis when you shop for food, and never go to a grocery store when you are hungry or anxious.

After meals, if you still feel hungry, use self-hypnosis to focus on a sense of inner fullness. Remember a perfect meal you once had, one where you didn't stuff yourself, where your stomach felt pleasantly full but not distended. You may have had a food hangover in the past, but now that you are learning to control your appetite, you feel better and healthier each day, all day.

If discouragement about losing the desired pounds rears its ugly head, relax and close your eyes. Using self-hypnosis, project a date on a screen in your mind and let that date represent the time you will achieve your desired weight. It may be six months from now, or it may be later than that. It might also be sooner. Let the date be a surprise to you, but whatever it is, that will be the day you can look forward to having the kind of body image you want.

Use at least one self-hypnotic session to concentrate on the exact place in your body where your hunger originates. It may be your stomach, your mouth, or your brain. Wherever it is, explore it and then practice increasing it and diminishing it, moving it from place to place, and anesthetizing it. This exercise will prove to you that you control your appetite; it doesn't control you. You learned long ago to control other urges, and you can control your hunger, too.

Plan a reward for what you will do for yourself when you have reached your desired weight. It may be a trip, a new wardrobe, or simply a feeling of satisfaction with yourself and your ability to control your life. Whatever your reward will be, use self-hypnosis to anticipate it, heightening the enjoyment and good feelings you have about working toward a healthy goal.

Aversion techniques, also known as negative conditioning, can help you avoid your favorite foods. Since they are similar to the stick in the carrot-and-stick analogy, I seldom use them, but many people find them helpful.

When you have trouble resisting temptation, use your hypnotic sessions to picture your favorite foods in your mind and then imagine them as something so disgusting that they lose their appeal for you. Make the association permanent, so that whenever you see or think about the tempting food, you immediately associate it with something revolting. For instance, if lemon meringue pie is your nemesis, picture the lemon filling in your mind as the yellow fat pathologists cut out in performing autopsies.

While using self-hypnosis for negative conditioning, you may want to project a parade of your favorite foods and see each of them as unappealing. Make up your own aversion techniques that are particularly nauseating or disgusting to you.

Posthypnotic suggestion can be a powerful tool for helping yourself control your appetite. To give yourself posthypnotic suggestions, simply go into a trance as deep as possible and repeat whatever suggestion you decide on over and over to yourself. You may also want to make a tape of your voice repeating it. Some possible examples of posthypnotic suggestions are:

"As my appetite lessens, I am enjoying my food more and more, feeling pride and pleasure in my ability to control my eating habits. As I eat less, I feel better and healthier, and I look like the person I want to be."

"Every time I see the refrigerator, I feel a sense of pride and inner calm, pride in myself for resisting the temptation to snack. The sight of the refrigerator will always make me feel this way, every time I see it."

"Every day, at the time I am most vulnerable to hunger attacks, I will become so busy with a project I enjoy that I won't think about my hunger or notice it in any way."

"My bathroom scales represent to me my commitment to lose weight, and every time I see the scales my commitment increases, since I know that stepping on them is now an enjoyable rather than a depressing experience. The sight of my scales will increase my desire to lose weight every time I see them."

Use guided imagery to reinforce your commitment. Now that you know your self-image is not overweight, give yourself a special hypnotic session every day to get to know the changed person you will be. See yourself in all the satisfying situations you will be encountering in your new shape.

Some of those might include seeing yourself in the dressing room of a clothing store, trying on new clothes without embarassment or guilt; seeing yourself at the beach in your bathing suit, knowing you look the way you want to look; seeing yourself at a party wearing the kinds of clothes that will show off your figure, not hide it.

Case Studies

Case One

The first thing Mrs. W. said to me when she came to my office was, "I just don't seem to have any will-power when it comes to dieting. I have managed to lose weight about four times in my life, but each time I gain it back within a few months, usually more than I had lost."

I could see that she was sincere and more than a little distraught over what she felt was a shameful inability to diet and maintain weight loss. She was a forty-year-old woman carrying around about thirty pounds of unnecessary flesh. Yet her clothes and grooming were neat and attractive. Only her face reflected her unhappiness.

"And you think I can help you?" I asked her.

"I hope so!" she laughed nervously. "My friend told me that she used hypnosis to lose weight and keep it off, and I figured it was worth a try."

"Is there something specific about your life now that makes you think this is the right time to lose weight permanently?" I asked.

"Well," she considered thoughtfully, "my kids are growing up now and they are more aware of me in a critical way. My husband has been teasing me a lot about my weight, too, and that makes me very uncomfortable. But mostly, I want to do it for myself. I'm sure that I will feel better if I do something about all this flab."

Her reasoning was clearly right. The most important

reason a person has for making any personal change is because it seems right for him or her. Changing yourself for the sake of others rarely works. Mrs. W. wanted to lose weight to please herself, and she did.

We had four sessions together, learning to induce self-hypnosis and discussing the techniques for weight loss and maintenance. During those four weeks she managed to lose eight pounds. She discovered that "having a weight problem" helped her feel weak and helpless, feelings she had suffered from all her life. A part of her wanted to be fat, wanted the easy solace of substituting overeating for dealing responsibly with some of her problems. However, she basically knew that this mental habit was left over from her youth and not really what she wanted now.

Mrs. W. used the technique of focusing on an active fantasy to induce hypnosis and saw herself in a bathing suit on a sandy beach, playing unself-consciously with her husband and children. She was able to subdue her appetite using this technique and others, concentrating on the rewards she would reap when she lost the un-wanted pounds.

Six months later I got a post card from Mrs. W., mailed from Jamaica. She wrote that the reality of her beach vacation surpassed even the fantasy she had enjoyed during the months of losing weight through self-hypnosis.

When she returned, she called me and spoke glowingly of the differences in her life now and her assurance that this time she could keep the weight off. "I have used self-hypnosis for other things, too, Doctor," she told me happily. "Not only am I slimmer and healthier, but I feel more relaxed on the job and at home than ever before!"

Her happy attitude stemmed from two things: her satisfaction in having lost the weight and her pleasure with her new body image and the new skill she had learned which gave her the key for real relaxation.

Case Two

Mr. J., a car salesman in a local display room, looked very unhappy when he came into my office. When I asked him how I could help him, he looked distinctly uncomfortable and said, "I hope you can help me lose some weight, Doc. My boss told me I was up for a promotion to office manager, but he made some negative remarks about my appearance. I got the message and now, I need help!"

Mr. J. weighed about 250 pounds, which he carried on a large frame. He also told me that he had read some articles recently about cholesterol and heart disease, and he was worried about his health since his father had died of a heart attack.

I was concerned about his motivation for losing weight, since the major focus seemed to be attached to his job and his boss's desire that he improve his appearance. But the concern for his health was genuine enough, so we proceeded to learn the techniques for self-hypnosis. He was an apt student and achieved a medium trance rather quickly.

We spent most of our five sessions working on self-analysis, and Mr. J. talked about how much he loved to cook and enjoy the fruits of his labor. Working in the kitchen relieved much of the loneliness he felt at living alone. He was proud of his ability to cook.

Under self-hypnosis, he revealed doubts about his ability to handle the added responsibility of managing the display room office, and he spoke quite happily of the satisfaction he found in salesmanship. He liked meeting people and getting to know them through his work, finding a great sense of pride in "being the best car salesman in this town." Ideomotor movements consistently revealed that he did not want to lose weight, that he was happy with his body image and liked the image of himself as a fat, jolly man.

After the fifth session, we discussed his case and Mr. J. came to the conclusion that he did not want the promotion his boss had offered him and would turn it down. He liked his life the way it was and didn't want to change either his job or his weight. So, I congratulated him on knowing his mind, and the last time I saw Mr. J., he seemed content with his decision.

Case Three

Mrs. C. sank down wearily in the chair next to my desk and immediately lit a cigarette. Blowing out a long stream of smoke, she sighed and said, "I don't know why I am here, really, I am probably just wasting your time."

"Why don't you tell me why you came?" I said encouragingly.

"Well, it's my weight. And don't tell me I am not

fat! I know I am not grotesquely overweight, but I think I am a tub!''

I smiled at her dramatic language and observed a slightly overweight thirty-two-year-old woman with an anxious look. She was fingering her sweater nervously, and I noticed she was trying to conceal a stain on her blouse.

''What has happened to you recently to make you want to lose weight?'' I asked.

She laughed, naturally and spontaneously. ''My clothes don't fit, and I hate the sight of myself in the mirror. My youngest child just turned three, and I think it is about time I stopped trying to convince myself that this extra weight is her fault!''

Mrs. C. went on to tell me that she was a full-time mother of two who was beginning to think about resuming her career as a librarian. Staying home with the children was rewarding, she explained, but lately she felt her life was dull and restrictive. The thought of going back to work had forced her to take a look at herself as her clients and colleagues would see her, and she could admit that she didn't like what she saw.

''I have always been an attractive person,'' she said honestly, ''but the years at home have turned me into a secret snacker. I'd like to learn how to control that and return to my regular weight.''

After Mrs. C. had learned the techniques of self-hypnosis, she discovered some important things about herself through self-analysis. Her mother had led her to believe that motherhood was a full-time, rewarding job, and although Mrs. C. believed that had been true for her mother, it didn't seem to be enough for her. She felt badly about that. One of the ways she coped with those guilty feelings was by overeating. She didn't deprive her children of anything, but neither did she want to sacrifice her life and happiness for them. One of the ways she tried to resolve this dilemma was by baking batch after batch of homemade cookies, which she doled out carefully to the children but gorged on herself.

Mrs. C. was quite puzzling to me for a period of time. It was hard to understand what it was that she needed or wanted. But gradually we both began to realize that she was facing a conflict between her need to gratify her own self-image of a competent and independent person and her feeling that her role was to stay home and be a traditional mother. Her own mother had been an overweight woman who encouraged her daughter to think for herself but had talked disdainfully about any woman who wasn't a "good cook and good mother."

So, to Mrs. C., food stains on her clothes were a badge of honor and femininity, and the extra pounds were proof that she was as nurturing a parent as her mother wanted her to be. This trap she had fallen into kept her bouncing back and forth between her image of her independent, clean, slender, neat self and her more earthy, chicken-soup mother self.

Mrs. C. realized how ineffective that kind of behavior was in resolving her anxieties, and she was finally able to realize that her mother's definition of a good mother and her own definition might be different. She

was then able to shed the ten pounds that made her
feel ugly and awkward, and, several months later, she
made adequate day-care arrangements for her children
and went back to library work happily and confidently.

6. Living Free of Cigarettes

Most people who walk into my smoking clinic begin by saying "I know smoking is bad and I want to stop. But, I can't seem to do it." I usually interrupt at this point and say, "I don't think smoking is bad." This tends to shock people. "But it is ruining my health!" they say, "and I know I should stop!" "I don't know if you should stop or not," I continue. "I view smoking as a choice that you make." Confusion reigns until I elaborate my philosophy about smoking.

Smoking is a behavior with many rewards. It obviously satisfies some deep need or people wouldn't keep smoking in the face of all the medical and social pressure against it. Like most behavior, it is the result of a value judgment. Just like the importance of money in your life, you have assigned a relative importance to smoking. If asked how much money you want to have, like most people, you will likely say "Millions!" But this isn't true. If it were, you would all be

85

studying finance, seriously playing the stock market, and so on. Money, like smoking, is important to you, but only relatively so. Closeness with others, leisure activities, intellectual pursuits, and children, for instance, might rank ahead of both the desire to make money and the desire to smoke. It is simply a question of choice.

Before you make that choice, you have to recognize its degree of importance to you. Only you can decide exactly how important any one thing in your life is to you. Just as each person alone must decide the issues of their lives, both consciously and unconsciously, so it is with smoking, drinking, taking drugs, or any other potentially damaging behavior.

It was Mark Twain who said, "Giving up smoking is easy; I've done it hundreds of times." Many people have made the superficial decision to quit smoking without understanding the hard work of finding out if the decision was deep and personally right for them. The person who quits without really wanting to stop can be exemplified by the woman whose husband bought her two cartons of cigarettes after she had been off them for two days, saying, "Here, smoke the damn things—I can't stand you without them!" Living free of cigarettes does not have to mean major personality changes brought on by feelings of deprivation or suffering, not if you are really in touch with why you want to quit.

Many people find themselves in a classic love-hate relationship with cigarettes. Perhaps you have stubbed out a half-smoked cigarette or crushed a whole pack in your hands, vowing, "Never again!" only to find yourself a few hours later cruising the streets in your car looking for an all-night cafe with a cigarette machine.

Smoking itself is neither good nor bad per se. It is simply a choice that you make after weighing the positive and negative rewards of tobacco. I do not believe that a person who continues to smoke is weak, bad, or any of the other pejorative terms commonly applied to smokers. We all have the right to choose whether or not we want to smoke, just as we have the right to decide how much sexual activity is necessary for us, or whether to play handball, watch TV, or follow sports.

Why People Choose to Smoke

Obviously, you have some reasons to keep smoking or you simply would not continue to do so. Some of the reasons for smoking I hear most often expressed are:

"Smoking gives me something to do with my hands."

"It calms me down."

"I like the taste."

"Smoking makes me feel confident about myself."

"It seems to dull my appetite, and I don't eat as much when I smoke."

"I like the excitement of a 'forbidden pleasure.' "

"It makes me look more mature, more sophisticated."

"A cigarette is the finishing touch on a good meal."

Psychiatrists and psychologists see other reasons, of course.

Oral Gratification

People hooked on cigarettes, say mental health experts, are seeking to relive those early sucking experiences at breast or bottle, or they are responding to the remembered comfort of a sucked thumb when fear or sadness struck as a child. As adults, some of us have replaced sucking on nipples or thumbs with sucking on cigarettes.

Stimulus/Response

The stimulus of tobacco produces for smokers the gratifying response of pleasure or relaxation. The sight of smoking paraphernalia or smoke floating upward has become inextricably associated with good feelings. Seeing a cigarette (stimulus) makes you want to smoke (response). All the steps along the way toward smoking are gratifying as is proved by the vast array of products designed to enhance the rituals of tobacco: leather pouches, gold lighters, slim silver cigarette cases, crystal ashtrays, ivory cigarette holders.

Sense of Inner Fullness

Occasionally, patients will relate an almost nirvana-like feeling of inner fullness when smoking. As their chests expand when smoke is inhaled, they speak of a pleasant sensation of warm gases flowing through their lungs and filling them with an enjoyment that is partially subliminal.

Expression of Anger and Revolt

For many people, smoking is a way to express anger against powerful others. Those who seem to chew their cigarettes or bite the ends of their pipes, for instance, are usually smoking out of a sense of anger. And we all use such expressions as "He burns me up," "I'd like to light into her," "I did a slow burn," or "Put that in your pipe and smoke it!"

Instantaneous Gratification

In addition to all the psychological reasons for smoking, there is an immediate physiological gratification involved in the process of inhaling tobacco. It releases glucose into the blood, lowers body temperature, raises energy levels, and relaxes the sympathetic nervous system.

Why People Choose Not to Smoke

There are as many reasons why people choose not to smoke or want to quit. Some of the most frequently heard are:

"It's dirty."

"It smells up the house (the car, the office)."

"Smoking is a fire hazard."

"My clothes and rugs and furniture are full of holes."

"It is too expensive."

"It dulls my taste buds."

"It makes my mouth feel like fourteen camels have passed through."

"My friends give me dirty looks when I light up."

"It stains my teeth and hands and fingers."

Those reasons are all valid and important, but for most people they pale in comparison to the medical facts about smoking. Even without the surgeon general's warning on every pack and carton, we all know beyond doubt that smoking is dangerous to our health.

Nothing about smoking is healthy. Medical students are routinely trained to get a "pack year history" from each patient as a reliable indicator of present health and future longevity. To figure out your pack year history, multiply the number of packs you smoke per day by the number of years you have been smoking. A person who has been smoking two packs a day for thirty years, for instance, has a sixty pack year history.

Chronic obstructive pulmonary disease (COPD) is automatically presumed to be present in anyone who has a greater than forty-five to fifty pack year history. COPD is, generally, a summation of all the effects of cigarette smoking and means that the lungs and bronchial passages have been damaged to the point where not enough air can be moved in and out of the lungs to fully oxygenate the blood. People with COPD suffer the same symptoms as those who live on mountain peaks. They are starved for air.

Other medical effects of smoking include emphysema, a condition which reduces the number of air cells in the lungs because of the chronic irritation of those cells by the elements present in cigarette smoke. The normal lung area, if all the tiny air cells were flattened and spread out, would be the size of a double tennis court. But smoking drastically reduces the number of air cells and gradually destroys much of the functioning lung area.

Also, smoking damages the epithelial lining of the bronchial tubes and forces the body to replace the lost cells. Often, atypical cells replace healthy ones as the bronchial lining struggles to cope with its injuries. Mucous membrane changes occur, too, an indication of the body's attempt to protect itself against the irritating elements of cigarette smoke. The more the cells are irritated, the more mucus is produced to protect the linings of the throat, bronchi, and lungs.

Other effects of smoking include chronic bronchitis with its attendant morning cough, sputum production (coughing up secretions of abnormal cells), hoarseness, chest pains, lessened resistance to colds, pneumonia, and viral infections.

Coincident with the pulmonary effects of smoking, there are well proven but less well understood correlations between smoking and other health problems such as heart attacks, strokes, childbirth difficulties, hypertension, arteriosclerosis, and hardening of the arteries.

And then there is the medical aspect of smoking that strikes the most fear in the most people: cancer. Smoking is a cause of cancer because the cellular irritation that takes place as a result of chronic inhalation of smoke often produces abnormal cells. Abnormal or atypical cells have a greater probability for becoming cancerous. Medical research has proven that anything that irritates normal cells long enough eventually leads to the production of more and more abnormal cells and, finally, to cancerous cells. Cancerous cells are markedly abnormal cells which reproduce themselves with lightning swiftness, and halting that reproduction is a difficult, painful, and too frequently futile process. Growths of abnormal cells are what we call cancer, and unchecked, they invade locally and spread to distant regions, usually causing the death of the organism. Cigarette smoking is linked not only to lung cancer, but also to cancer of the mouth, lips, throat, and tongue.

All this medical evidence is of cold comfort to the person in a lonely struggle to give up those very addicting little tubes of tobacco. Logically and intellectually, no one can deny that smoking is harmful, yet logic and reason are often not enough to overcome a consuming addiction. This is where hypnosis comes in as a powerful aid to learning to live a cigarette-free life, *if* that is *your* desire.

Autoanalysis

For many people, understanding the reasons why they smoke can be the first step toward living a tobacco-free life. Take some time under self-hypnosis to give some thought to your individual reasons for smoking.

Under hypnosis, take a package of cigarettes in your hands and see what it means to you. How does it feel?

Explore the package using all available senses. Look at the writing on the package, the color and shape; feel the cellophane crackling under your fingers, the angles and shape of the pack as you turn it over in your hands. Smell it, and then allow your mind to be open to your associations about smoking. Ask yourself why you have this strange craving and dependence on such seemingly neutral objects.

Under hypnosis, take out a cigarette, hold it and feel it, look at it and smell it, then put it between your lips. Consider lighting it, then put it down and see what associations come to mind again. If you found any of the reasons for smoking discussed in the beginning of this chapter to apply to you, try to understand them now in a deeper and more meaningful way.

Under hypnosis, pick up the cigarette again and put it between your lips. Focus your concentration on the feelings that come to mind as you experience the sensation of putting a cigarette in your mouth. Then pay close attention to everything you do as you light it. Focus on the act of striking a match or flipping a lighter, and as you do it, notice what these actions seem to represent to you. Inhale that first puff of smoke and concentrate on what it feels like for you as the smoke enters your bronchial passages and lungs. Do you feel a sense of inner fullness? Try to picture how the smoke travels through your body. Do you feel that you are polluting your body? Concentrate on these sensations and what they seem to mean for you. Then stub out the cigarette, again focusing and concentrating on that act and noticing any associations or feelings that might help you understand why smoking is important to you.

Under hypnosis, ask yourself some questions. What significant others in my life are smokers? How do I feel about the people I know who smoke (admiration, respect, disappointment, anger)? Why are cigarettes so important to me? What do I need that cigarettes give me? Do I still need it, whatever it is? Is smoking a part of my life that I want to retain? Would a cigarette-free existence be pleasant? What rewards would I get out of being cigarette-free?

At this point, it is possible that you will decide your smoking behavior is of real value to you, something you want to cherish and keep. It is, after all, your own business, and you have the right to decide.

Assuming that you have decided to live cigarette free, see how this decision feels under hypnosis. Check it out with your unconscious to see if it feels right. Use the ideomotor movement technique discussed in chapter 5. Make your right index finger represent "yes," your left index finger "no." Your right thumb will be "I don't know," and your left thumb "I don't wish to answer." Relax under self-hypnosis and say to yourself, "I have made a conscious decision to live a cigarette-free life, and can support this at all levels of my consciousness." Frame this as a hypnotic question and, using ideomotor movements, wait for a response.

If you get a positive reply, you have strong inner evidence that your decision is based both on your conscious wishes and your unconscious forces. If the reply is not forthcoming or is negative, then go ahead and proceed with the program, understanding that you will have to use more conscious effort and that you probably have some unconscious, unresolved needs to gratify yourself with cigarettes.

You can override these objections if you wish. Or, you can go back to step one and reanalyze your smoking behavior and feelings to see if you have left anything out. For some people, the simple and unilateral conscious decision to quit, firmly made, makes the whole process rather easy. For others, more work and self-analysis are necessary to gain the rewards of a tobacco-free life.

If you are a person who has succeeded in the past at giving up cigarettes only to return to the habit, use hypnosis to go over the events in the past that led you to quit. Examine the motives that convinced you back then, and think about what your life was like when you didn't smoke. Then try to understand why you started again. Was there a specific event or urge that made you return to cigarettes? Use self-hypnosis to project yourself backwards in time and see if you can gain some new insights into why you returned to smoking.

When you have examined your smoking behavior and reexamined the feelings or events that led you to stop smoking in the past, give yourself some time under self-hypnosis to analyze your thoughts about your decision to live cigarette free now. Have you framed your decision as ''I have decided to *try* to live tobacco free''? If so, you will discover under autoanalysis that you have left the door wide open to begin smoking again sometime in the future. Attempt to recognize your ambivalence and the escape hatch you have given yourself and spend some more time making your decision. *Trying* to stop smoking is like *trying* to convince the sun to stop rising. Either continue to enjoy smoking or decide to live free of cigarettes forever.

Techniques

For the person who is going to live free of cigarettes and the noxious gases in their lungs and nose, the following techniques are offered to help make the experience easier and more rewarding. Choose the technique that most suits your needs. Master one or several of the techniques, and then feel free to invent your own variations to suit your personality and habits.

Panic Control

To some people, living free of cigarettes is just a catchy way of saying, "I am going to have to give up smoking." That means a loss. There is no doubt that quitting can be a loss, the loss of the ability to reach in your shirt pocket or purse and always find what you need. It is going to be gone. The comfortable habit of going through the rituals of smoking is lost forever. It is okay to mourn this loss, just as you would the loss of friendship, position, a loved one, or a treasured heirloom. There may be a well-controlled but obvious feeling of panic.

Since you have decided that cigarettes are no longer

available, see if there is a feeling of unease lurking below your surface. Spend some time under hypnosis getting yourself familiar with that panicky feeling. Go ahead and see how it feels. You might see yourself later on tonight groping through your clothes for an old dried-out pack of cigarettes. See if this panic is uncontrollable, stronger than you are. Perhaps it isn't. The secret here, of course, is that knowing the enemy is half the battle.

Build yourself what psychologists call a hierarchy of fears. Start with the mildest. It might be the fear that later on today you will spend some time searching frantically for a cigarette. Somewhere in the middle of your hierarchy of fears, you might imagine that you will see a friend light up and be unable to resist the temptation to do likewise. The most helpless or fearful feeling might crop up at the next party you attend or the next time you fight with your mate.

Make up your own continuum of fear and expectations of the terrible things that will happen to you without those all-powerful cigarettes. Under hypnosis, put yourself in each of those situations, starting out with the least threatening. As you do so, feel and anticipate the experience, then relax, feel the confidence you have learned to know under hypnosis, the comfortable feeling of power and mastery. Turn your panic into a friend who is going to help you do what you want to do. Sometimes it is helpful to do this so much that you frankly get bored with the panic and it loses its power over you.

Mini-Relaxation

Every time you notice a desire for a cigarette, quickly, in a few seconds, go through a mini-relaxation: drop your shoulders, exhale, and turn off the cigarette urge. This is a technique that can be learned in a variety of ways. Practice every time you want a cigarette and reward yourself with a quick, instant relaxation. Perhaps you might want to accompany this good feeling with the phrase, "I don't want it; it has no power over me."

With this technique, the multiple little urges to smoke don't add up through the days and weeks when you are learning to enjoy being cigarette free, because you have taken care of them as they arrive. This involves, of course, being aware of your cigarette urges. Watch for these mini-urges that come on, for instance when the phone rings, when you see someone else light up, or after a good meal.

Replacing Loss

Plan to schedule several hypnotic sessions throughout the day with each one designed to give you a sense of peaceful relaxation and comfort to replace the loss of a hugely valued but dangerous friend: cigarettes. The two techniques perhaps best suited for this purpose are progressive muscular relaxation and focusing on a physiological act. You will probably want to choose to focus on the physiological act of respiration, concentrating on filling your lungs with cool, clean air and enjoying the sensation of cleansing your lungs with pure air instead of tobacco fumes.

Substitution Rewards

Every time you feel a desire to smoke begin to surface, use hypnosis to substitute pleasure for cigarettes. The kinds of pleasure you choose to substitute may fall into several categories.

PSYCHIC

Under hypnosis, think of a particularly pleasing psychic reward you would like to receive for your healthful behavior. Maybe you will choose to concentrate on feeling more mature than those who continue to smoke. Each time you want a cigarette congratulate yourself instead on the mature behavior of eliminating an unhealthy habit. There are many types of psychic rewards you can give yourself in place of your tobacco dependence, such as allowing yourself a warm feeling of being loved or a feeling of satisfaction at being able to control your harmful urge to smoke.

PHYSIOLOGICAL

Physiological rewards might include substituting an artificial cigarette, a nonexistent cigarette, to gain a similar physiological sense of pleasure. To do this, simply allow your hand to touch your lips in a casual, off-hand manner. At the same time, take a drag of cool, clean air and blow it out, feeling the gratification in your trachea, larynx, and lungs. Puffing cool, clean air from a phantom cigarette is pleasant to many people and is especially useful as an emergency procedure in times of stress, as when you are feeling particularly deprived and think, "I might as well smoke; I have nothing else." As you enjoy the pleasure of your nonexistent cigarette, remind yourself that what you have now is a better chance for a long and healthy life.

TANGIBLE

You might want to plan a tangible reward for yourself with the money you will save by not buying cigarettes. Figure out how much you would spend on tobacco products for a period of, say two months, and then plan a tangible reward you will buy at the end of that time. Use hypnosis as a way to anticipate your reward.

Negative Conditioning

Negative conditioning employs useful and powerful techniques that involve avoidance behavior. It is up to you to decide whether or not you want to use them. Some suggestions are listed below that you can use as take-off points to make up your own negative conditioning techniques using situations that are particularly unpleasant or revolting to you.

Make yourself comfortable and enter a hypnotic state quickly. Visualize an ashtray filled with cigarette butts and ashes. You may want to actually smell an ashtray before you go into this so the memory is vivid. Then imagine this junk in your lungs. See the dirtiness and smelliness of the ashtray and imagine how the contents of it would feel in your lungs, visualizing the dry, nasty ashes and the stickiness of the nicotine secretions in your lungs, choking you.

Whether you have seen pictures of smokers' lungs or not, go ahead and form a mental picture of your lungs, concentrating on the thick mucous secretion in your air passages stained yellow with nicotine. Continue to visualize your lungs as they would be if you kept on smoking—gradually developing more dead air space. Let this picture stay with you whenever you feel the urge to smoke.

Direct Suggestion

Induce hypnosis as deeply as possible and give yourself suggestions, attempting to direct them at your deepest levels of consciousness and unconsciousness. Repeat firmly to yourself, "I am free of cigarettes. I am free of the desire for cigarettes." Repetition of this should be often, and the results will be directly proportionate to your efforts. Repeat this statement at least three times daily over a period of weeks to get the maximum benefits. You can make up your own suggestions, of course, ones that fit your own situation. Another phrase you might use is "I control tobacco; tobacco doesn't control me."

Posthypnotic Suggestion

Posthypnotic suggestion is the technique most favored by smoking clinics, one for which you can pay from $30 to $300. Smoking clinics begin by discussing at length all the reasons why smoking is harmful.

Finally, hypnosis is induced by the facilitator to a level where posthypnotic suggestion can take effect. You have already learned how to hypnotize yourself to this level of suggestibility, and you can now tailor your posthypnotic suggestions to fit your needs. Many people report success by keeping their instructions as simple as possible: "I will not smoke cigarettes, buy them, nor accept them. If I did, I would be unable to light one and automatically would break it in half." Repetition of this suggestion is important. Use this technique every time you practice hypnosis, and repeat the chosen phrase several times with clarity, emphasis, and firmness.

Case Histories

Case One

Ms. W. was a thirty-one-year-old woman with a thirteen pack year history of smoking. She readily admitted that she came to the smoking clinic as much out of curiosity about hypnosis as a desire to quit smoking. Since her expectations about hypnosis were high and her motivation to live tobacco-free seemed genuine, I expected she would have no trouble giving up what she considered to be an unhealthy and unsatisfying habit.

She had begun smoking at the age of fifteen, enjoying the feeling of acting contrary to her parents' wishes, but related that her mother soon discovered what she was doing and protested not against the smoking itself, but the sneaky behavior of hiding the fact. Her mother then gave her permission to smoke at home, which Ms. W. resented, since it took a lot of the fun out of what had been a forbidden pleasure.

Still, Ms. W. continued to smoke, but was never completely happy about it. She expressed irritation with the rites and rituals of smoking and disliked having to keep tabs on her cigarettes and lighters and empty ashtrays. She hated the way her mouth felt in the morning, she said, and the way the smell of smoke clung to her hair and clothes. Her husband did not smoke and her children were beginning to react to the antismoking propaganda on TV, asking their mother to please quit.

Ms. W. seemed to have every reason to stop, and I was frankly surprised when, week after week of the group meeting, she reported that she was still smoking. She had been so articulate about her reasons for wanting to quit, that I finally asked her why she *wanted* to smoke. "I think it is purely a physical addiction," she said thoughtfully. "My body seems to need whatever it is nicotine provides."

She went on to explain that her smoking behavior was slightly unusual in that she never smoked until late afternoon, finding the thought of cigarettes before noon extremely unpleasant. She had given up cigarettes in the past, once for as long as two and a half years when pregnancy had made the idea of cigarettes disgusting. She was angry with herself for starting to smoke again, but didn't wish to get pregnant in order to quit again.

One week, Ms. W. revealed that, using self-analysis,

she had realized suddenly that her smoking behavior was connected with her feelings about her work. A fulltime mother for the past seven years, she had recently begun to write seriously again. About the same time she started smoking once more. Under self-hypnosis, she connected this with the fact that she spent her morning, nonsmoking hours doing housework and childcare, work she felt quite confident about doing well. She reserved late afternoons and evenings for writing (and smoking). She decided that smoking represented for her the way she had tried to cover her adolescent fears and uncertainties, and that she was using smoking now to calm her anxieties about her ability to be a success as a writer.

She was sure there was more to it than that, but she was delighted with her discovery and went on to use the technique of replacing loss of tobacco as an anxiety reliever with the relaxing sense of calmness and confidence she found under hypnosis. When the urge to smoke hit her in the afternoon, she took time out from writing for a session of self-hypnosis and returned to the typewriter with renewed confidence in her talent.

But first, she had decided to pick a date to begin her cigarette-free life and had awakened that day to a sense of freedom and anticipation of a more healthy life. She spent the first morning washing her hair, washing all the curtains in her house, washing, polishing, and putting away all the ashtrays, and generally setting up a situation that would make quitting a more pleasant and rewarding experience.

Six months later, Ms. W. told me that the urge to

smoke rarely came up any more, but that she was using self-hypnosis regularly for relaxation and a sense
of increased creativity.

Case Two

Ms. K., a forty-five-year-old, moderately obese
woman, contacted me for help with both her hypertension and her smoking habits. The internal medicine
clinic at the large teaching hospital where I was working referred her to me because she seemed an ideal
candidate for some research we were doing on hypertension and hypnosis.

Hypertension is chronically elevated blood pressure
that causes eventual damage to the kidneys, heart, and
other organs, and can precipitate heart attacks and
strokes. It is difficult to diagnose hypertension because
it is a symptom-free illness except in its last stages.
This is one of the reasons why it is important to have
regular blood pressure readings taken.

Psychic tension is one of the causes of constriction
of the blood vessels and elevated blood pressure. In
many types of hypertension, controlling psychic tension through hypnosis lowers blood pressure and
checks the disease.

"I'm a very tense person," Ms. K. said over the
phone when we first talked. "I have always been that
way and lately it seems worse. I am smoking more,
too. In fact, I'm the original smoking-more-now-and-
enjoying-it-less person!"

I described the research we were doing and asked if
she would agree to having her first session attended by

a group of residents and interns who were interested in the clinical use of hypnosis as treatment for hypertension. She agreed, and went on to add that one session was all she would be able to attend before leaving town on an extended business trip.

Under these unusual circumstances, I ushered Ms. K. into a small amphitheater, where we both put on microphones and proceeded to talk about her problems in front of the audience. Ms. K. explained that she held a high level administrative job with the local school district. She felt a lot of on-the-job pressure and suspected that fact was partly responsible for her increased hypertension. In the past, her condition had been somewhat relieved by diuretics, but she had gradually been forced to take more potent antihypertension medication.

Not only was she feeling pressure at work, she went on to say, but her chain smoking had become another real problem. She had a fifty pack year history of smoking and was particularly concerned because an aunt had died of lung cancer six months earlier.

Her smoking behavior, she felt, was a direct result of the tension she felt at work, and she related that she chain-smoked two packs a day. "But," she laughed, "I really don't smoke two packs a day because most of them burn up in the ashtray!"

When I asked her to elaborate more on the pressures she felt in her life, she sighed. "I am under as much pressure at home as at work," she said. "We have five children, and they demand a lot of time. I always thought that this stage of my life would be pleasant and easy, now that the kids are growing up and I have reached a position of authority in my work. But I don't even have time to ride my horse any more, and the only time I get to spend with my husband is when he drives us both into work every morning.''

As I saw it, Ms. K. had three major problems, all of which were interrelated: hypertension, smoking, and mild obesity. As always, in a case like this where the starting point isn't clear, I asked her to tell me where she would like to begin.

She said her main goals were to stop smoking, control her hypertension, and not gain weight while doing it. "I have to admit," she said forthrightly, "that I doubt you can help me in the short time we have today. And I really don't see the connection between hypnosis and changing my behavior."

I explained that, for her, hypnosis would probably be a state of increased focus of energy as well as body relaxation. Comparing it to good study habits, a discipline with which she was already familiar, I elaborated on how good hypnotic techniques would help her alter her physiological functions (hypertension) as well as her habits (smoking).

We decided to limit our objectives to stopping smoking without gaining weight and to see what effect that would have on her hypertension. This made sense to Ms. K., and since we had only thirty minutes left to get her started on her own course of self-hypnosis, I asked her to tell me the most relaxing thing she could think of. "That is easy," she replied. "I am the most relaxed on horseback, cantering along a ridge trail overlooking the ocean." She began to relax markedly as she described her favorite leisure activity.

Using the technique of active fantasy, I asked Ms. K. to close her eyes, allowing her shoulders to drop and her body to relax while she thought about riding her horse. She was instructed to re-experience everything about that ride, to see again the sun gleaming on the ocean, to feel the movement of riding, to smell the fresh air and the salt spray. Allowing herself to relive this pleasant experience, one she had not allowed herself to have recently, Ms. K.'s respiration slowed perceptively and the muscles in her face relaxed as she went into a light hypnotic trance.

To the students in the amphitheater, it looked as though I was hypnotizing Ms. K., but, of course, we know that she was doing it herself. Shown the technique of active fantasy and with further practice, she would be able to recreate the hypnotic state on her own whenever she wished.

When she was fully alert again, she discussed her experience and repeated her concern that, while she had found hypnosis relaxing, she was having trouble making the connection between relaxation and changing her habits. I asked her if she had thought about smoking while under hypnosis, and she replied that she had not. I then repeated that what she chose to do with her new skill was up to her, but that she would find her own ways of using it to effect the changes she wanted. This was an important concept for Ms. K. because she was a person who insisted on doing things for herself.

Two weeks later, she called long distance to report that it was working. She had quit smoking without any problem, but found that she was gaining weight. I suggested she use hypnosis to slow down her eating, a useful way she could control her calorie intake as well as get some relief for her hypertensive condition.

The next time I saw her, a few weeks after she returned from her trip, she told me that she was practicing self-hypnosis regularly and had not had a cigarette since the first time we met. She had decreased her blood pressure significantly, and although she still required medication for her hypertension, she was able to get better results with lower doses. Then she told me the hypnotic technique she had developed which she said had made a remarkable difference in her life. She now used self-hypnosis every morning in the car as her husband drove them into work. She spent her commuting time inducing and enjoying a hypnotic trance, imagining herself on her horse, relaxing deeply and, as she put it, "setting the tone for my entire day. It has made a tremendous difference in the way I feel at work and at home. There is just one problem! My husband now wants me to share the driving so he can do the same thing!"

Case Three

Dr. Z., one of the medical residents who was present at Ms. K.'s induction, sought me out a few days later. We sat down in my office and he told me he wanted to stop smoking and to use hypnosis to make the process less painful.

"I have read about hypnosis, of course," he said, "but it never occurred to me to use it to quit smoking. Now I want to try. What is the best technique to use?"

"That depends on a lot of things," I told him. "Why do you want to stop now?"

"Mostly because I cannot afford it," he grinned, "but also because my wife just had a baby, and every time I look at my daughter I realize I want to be around to watch her grow up."

Dr. Z. was a dedicated, intense kind of person who seemed to approach life and its problems in a direct, logical manner. He viewed problem solving as a challenge, and enjoyed the rational, step-by-step process toward finding solutions. I suggested he use self-hypnosis for autoanalysis before giving up smoking, but I suspected he would bypass that route, especially since, at his insistence, the bulk of our conversation was about several techniques he could use to kick the habit.

He returned to my office a few weeks later and told me what he had done so far. "I went home that night," he said, "and practiced for about an hour. I used eye fixation in combination with Jacobsonian relaxation (progressive muscular relaxation) and I think I achieved a medium trance. Then I used direct suggestion to tell myself I was no longer going to smoke. I repeated it over and over until it felt like a chant. I didn't smoke the next day or the next day, and I kept on practicing. In a few days, I thought I was ready for some posthypnotic suggestions, so I told myself I would no longer be able to buy cigarettes, and if I did pick one up I would break it in half. I kept repeating that suggestion, along with my chant."

"Well," I asked, "how is it going now?"

"It works," he said firmly. "But I have discovered that I am really quite a cagey character."

"What happened?"

"A week ago, an old medical school buddy of mine came through town and we went to a bar after work. I had a few beers with my friend, and I found myself dying to smoke. I decided a few cigarettes wouldn't hurt anything, but when I got up to go buy a pack, I found I just couldn't do it! It was weird, really strange." He paused. "So I asked the bartender to buy me a pack, and I had to tip him two dollars to do it!"

I laughed. "You found a way to get around yourself, I see."

"That is not all. When I finally had the pack of cigarettes, I opened it and took one out. Without even thinking about it, I broke it in half before I could light it. My friend thought I was crazy. So did I. I broke three cigarettes before I finally got one lit, and I have been smoking ever since."

"Did you try autoanalysis?"

"No, I thought I knew why I smoked. Relaxation and habit."

"Probably that is not all there is to it. Why don't you try using hypnosis to figure out some of the other reasons. You could start with why you wanted a cigarette so badly that night." He agreed to do so and the next time I saw him he was eager to report his success.

"I think I have got it figured out now," he told me. "I devoted a couple of sessions to self-analysis of my smoking behavior and I learned that the reason I started smoking that night went all the way back to the reason I started smoking in the first place. I have always felt a little uneasy in social situations, like a long-tailed cat in a room full of rocking chairs. Smoking was one way to defuse that anxiety. It gave me something to do, something that eased that sense of anxiety.''

''That sounds reasonable.''

''I thought so, too. So, what I am doing now is using self-hypnosis to anticipate the feeling of social unease and then deal with it on the spot, relaxing and letting that relaxation replace the need for a cigarette. I think I will be able to handle it better the next time I find myself in that situation.''

Dr. Z. had a right to be pleased with himself, since he had some success, followed by a set-back, followed by a deeper understanding of his behavior. He was confident that he could tackle his next temptation more creatively.

7. Controlling Pain

Nobody gets through life without experiencing pain. Pain is democratic; it strikes the king as often as the beggar. Pain should not be ignored, but neither does it have to darken your days or be the center around which your life revolves.

Let us take a personal look at pain. Pinch yourself on your left thigh. Now try to define what you feel. Try to put it into words. Most likely, you will describe it circularly: a pinching sensation in my left thigh.

Now pinch yourself on your right thigh. This time, try to notice exactly what that sensation feels like. The first thing you will feel is the anticipation of pain as your fingers hover over your thigh. Next, as you pinch, you will feel the sensation begin to build, localized at a particular spot. There will be a certain emotional attitude about that sensation, a change in the quality of the sensation, and a gradual lessening until it disappears with only a few lingering aftersensations.

What you have just experienced is so common as to be almost beneath notice. Pain is a part of everyday life, something to which we often pay only scant attention. But pain is a combination of many things:

1. The anticipation of pain.
2. The physical sensation.
3. The social quality.
4. The emotional set.
5. The biological aspect.
6. The cultural/historical aspect.

Before we look individually at these six aspects of pain, a word of warning is in order. No pain should be ignored, and hypnosis should not be used to mask the body's natural warning signal of disease or injury. Too, if most of your life is spent in psychic pain, then psychotherapy should be considered. Hypnosis can be used as an adjunctive aid to diagnosis and treatment; it is not a panacea for all ills.

The Anticipation of Pain

The anticipation of pain is that feeling you get on the way to the dentist, especially when you know the painkilling drug isn't going to work and the drill gets closer and closer to the nerve cavity. Anticipation has always been an important aspect of pain. The German Gestapo in World War II, for instance, made it a point to let the victim know in advance that more and more pain would be inflicted until the desired results were obtained. Thinking about pain, waiting for it to hit, bracing oneself for the onslaught—all these are the overture to pain itself.

Many patients with chronic lower back pain tell me that their first thought of the day is dread of the agony ahead. The migraine sufferer is well aware of the anticipation of the sick headache, and many patients describe the painless "aura" that precedes the onset of the headache. The aura itself doesn't hurt, but the migraine sufferer, knowing what is coming, feels sick when the signal arrives.

One terminal cancer patient treated by Milton Erikson, physician and hypnotist, had excruciating bouts of pain every twenty to thirty minutes which lasted only a few seconds. The technique used by Dr. Erikson in that case involved inducing a posthypnotic suggestion of amnesia for the pain. Until then, the patient had been in constant distress, lying rigid in bed waiting for the next spasm of pain. After the hypnotic treatment, the man still had the brief, intense pains, about thirty minutes apart, but he forgot them immediately. It was this that made his situation bearable and allowed him to have a dignified and relatively comfortable last few weeks. Hypnotic amnesia eliminated both his anticipation of pain and his dependence on large doses of morphine, which fogged his mind and clouded his days.

Anticipation of pain is, of course, also a learning tool and keeps children from touching hot stoves and adults from picking fights with longshoremen. But anticipation carried to extremes is useless suffering.

The Physical Sensation of Pain

Many people I see in the pain clinic can't describe
their pain. They can't even locate it. One patient who
had been troubled by headaches for over twenty years
could only describe her pain as "it makes me feel
sick." Others can pinpoint it exactly. "It is right behind my eyes," a migraine sufferer told me, "and
then it rolls around to cover my whole head like a
mist."

The physical sensation of pain can encompass many
feelings. It may be sharp, dull, throbbing, steady, intense, burning, aching, or stabbing. If you have talked
about your pain, perhaps someone has said or indicated to you that "it is all in your head." For your
purposes, pain is where you find it. *All pain is real.*
It is something you feel and something that can be
quantified only by you, the person experiencing it.

One doctor told me, "If I can't find a cause for their
headaches, then they don't have them!" This may have
helped him deal with his own ambiguities about pain,
but it didn't help his patients much. Pain is a subjective experience that has to be approached individually.
If you say you hurt right *there*, then it hurts right *there*,
no matter what anyone else tells you.

The Social Quality of Pain

Social conditioning influences the way we cope with
our pain. All our lives we are taught that:

1. *Pain is something that is out of our control.* The experience of pain for most Americans is entirely passive. From early childhood we learn to take our pain to others for treatment; to our parents, the school nurse, doctors. Decisions about our pain are often made without consulting us. Many doctors will routinely prescribe pain medication without even asking the patient how much pain he or she has. I am often pleased, in emergency room work, to hear patients with severe injuries refuse medication when I ask if they want it. Many will say with a smile, "I don't think I need it." They seem to be reassuring me that they can handle their pain.

2. *Pain has a certain quantum.* It ranges from the minor pain of a stubbed toe, through the more serious pain of a broken arm, all the way to the agony of second degree burns or worse. We learn to react accordingly, saving our loudest groans for the most severe pain. One woman told me that she was astonished when in labor with her first child to hear the nurse announce it was time to go to the delivery room. "I remember thinking," she told me, "that this couldn't be all! I was waiting for the pain to get unbearable. That is what I expected, but it didn't happen."

3. *Pain is either to be treated or endured, nothing in between.* Treatment varies from hugs and kisses, rubbing and ice packs, to aspirin, Demerol, or morphine. Endurance means putting up with pain, living with it, sometimes even embracing it as a way of life.

The Emotional Set of Pain

Pain can trigger all sorts of reactions: fear, uncertainty, anger, resignation. And different kinds of pain evoke different reactions. For instance, the pain you felt when you pinched yourself would be entirely different if someone else had been doing the pinching. Fear and uncertainty would be added to the pain equation, and this might either increase or mask the physical sensation. Many people who suffer chronic pain, such as lower back pain or arthritis, report that their anger at their disability affects their perception of the experience.

Your immediate circumstances at the onset of pain also affect your emotional reaction. If you are depressed when pain strikes, you will probably feel it more. If you stub your toe running home with the news you have just won the state lottery, you may not even notice. Exhilaration usually dulls pain while depression enhances it.

One of the most overlooked aspects of pain in modern medicine is suffering. After all, disease is just that: disease, a loss of feeling of comfort. Intense pain is bearable if suffering does not accompany it. There are many examples of this phenomenon. People who work on cancer wards will tell you that doctors who are sympathetic, warm, and open, who spend time explaining the unknown, often have "better patients." Relieving the fear of the unknown in a human, sympathetic way decreases suffering, and the result is less requirement for pain medication.

Another example has been discovered on battlefields. A surgeon at Iwo Jima in World War II noted that even severely wounded marines seldom asked for morphine. The great relief of being removed from that maelstrom of death and terror allowed the wounded to be almost without pain. Even though they were hurt, their wounds meant a hospital ship, clean sheets, and a ticket home.

Many women who have prepared for childbirth will attest to this phenomenon, too. Instead of seeing it as the "Curse of Eve," they find prepared childbirth thrilling and exhilarating and require little or no pain medication during delivery. They also recover faster.

The modern pain sufferer is just that: a sufferer. By decreasing suffering and uncertainty, pain becomes less crippling.

The Biological Aspect of Pain

To the modern neurophysiologist, pain is a nervous discharge initiated at a peripheral pain receptor and transmitted by biochemical-electrical means down certain nerves into the spinal cord. There it makes connections, called synapses, with neurons (nerve cells) in the central nervous system. It then is conducted upward to the various centers in the brain, usually the thalamus, from which it is transmitted by further biochemical-electrical conduction to higher brain centers, called association centers. Eventually, the nervous discharge called pain reaches the cortex of the brain where it becomes conscious.

This has been thought to be a process that occurred

without regulation. Recently, though, the gate theory of pain was developed in an attempt to explain why some stimuli were felt as pain and others weren't. For example, some scratching feels okay, but too much is painful. Neurons that send pain up the spinal cord are like gates that can be opened or shut. Some types of sensations (electrical discharges) reaching them will not open the gate (like scratching a little), while another combination of electrical input *will* open the gate (like scratching a lot).

Lately, some fascinating discoveries in neurochemistry have shown that very potent chemicals, endorphins and enkephalins, are produced in the brain and travel down the spinal cord to the area where the pain neurons make their first connections. These chemicals are similar to morphine in structure and may be the first key to understanding how humans can selectively turn off pain. This bit of modern knowledge may explain how the shaman did his stuff. Just as the witch doctor didn't need to know chemistry to relieve suffering, neither does the modern patient have to have an M.D. to decrease pain.

The biological pursuit of pain has perhaps led to ignorance. In finding more and more effective drugs, we may have learned to be technicians rather than healers. Since drugs work so well and so rapidly in many ways to relieve pain, most modern Americans are given a prescription when they complain of pain.

Many doctors today will deny that there is any human element in pain at all, the old if-I-can't-see-it-it-ain't-there approach to medicine. Too often, patients are approached as if they were cars with broken parts.

Of course, the inability to find a pathological cause for pain leaves both the doctor and patient feeling frustrated and impotent. People have more or less forgotten that for thousands of years humankind controlled and perhaps cured pain without pills, surgery, or injections. For us to relearn those premedical skills is part of the reason for this book.

The Cultural/Historical Aspect of Pain

In the most remote history, pain and the avoidance of pain serve primitive organisms as a means of survival and an aid to reproduction. A simple flatworm, for example, will avoid heat and acid environments: its primitive nervous system keeps it in a living space that is safe. A flatworm that didn't feel pain (i.e., a too warm environment) would probably not survive to reproduce. Pain is the mechanism that insures safety.

For higher animals, pain involves suffering as well as a nervous discharge. For human beings, pain and its avoidance can rightly be viewed as a way of improving the quality of life. Early people learned to build better shelters and use fire to avoid the suffering of being cold. Pain was an educational tool for our ancestors, as it is for us.

In the early tribal stage, humankind developed a complex system for quantifying and controlling pain. The shaman of yesterday had certain rituals to perform and certain spirits to appease. He or she used herbs, magic, rituals, and incantations. Shamans enjoyed remarkable success and their failures were explained away by the patient's having angered a god beyond redemption. How did witch doctors cure pain? The answer is simple: a highly developed organism like a human being has the innate capacity built into its neuro-physiological system to turn up or turn down its pain threshold.

By replacing superstition with a deeper understanding of the physical and chemical workings of our bodies and minds, modern medicine is turning shamanism into science. Pain is a remnant of a primitive biological system, a survival mechanism that works as well today as it ever did, but can get out of control. It is still necessary for us as organisms, but it can pass the point of usefulness for an individual.

This chapter can help you learn what that point of usefulness is for you.

Autoanalysis

Each of the six aspects of pain just discussed are as individual to you as your own fingerprints. In the light of this discussion, you take some time now to analyze your personality-pain profile. Understanding your pain and your individual reaction to it can give you the tools to custom tailor your conquest of this unwelcome companion.

Before attempting to use self-hypnosis as a way to control pain, it might be useful to keep a pain log for a period of time, perhaps a week or more. Jot down everything you notice about your pain, when it occurs, what you are doing when it strikes, how it feels, where you are, what time it is, who you are with, and so on. Any and every detail you can observe about your pain behavior can provide valuable clues for you to use in your self-analytic sessions. Study your log before beginning, and then use whatever hypnotic technique works best for you. We are going to try to analyze your pain and your relationship to it.

1. Is pain an integral part of you life? Have you come to expect pain as a regular visitor? Take some time now to think about your pain. Where is it coming from? Where is it located? What kind of quality does it have? Tell yourself about your pain—is it sharp, dull, burning, constant?

2. What other feelings are hooked up with your pain? Do nausea, aching, or a feeling of helplessness enter into the picture? Is your pain something that has to be endured? Is it out of your control?

3. What relationship does pain have to your life? Look for patterns that may have developed around your pain and your pain behavior.

4. What does pain keep you from doing that you would ordinarily have to do? Does normal life stop when pain strikes?

5. What does pain cause you to do that you wouldn't do otherwise? Examine your typical behavior at the onset of pain. Where do you go and what steps do you take to cope with it?

6. Has pain become a large part of your conversation? Do you talk about it a lot? If so, to whom do you talk and do they listen? What feedback do you get from others about your pain? Do they view you with sympathy or skepticism?

7. Think about how your parents handled pain. Did either of your parents suffer the same pain you are experiencing? Were there any rewards in being sick as a child (comic books, unlimited TV, etc.)? Are there any patterns or emerging connections between past and present pain behavior?

8. Can you imagine your life without your pain? Close your eyes and see what changes would be involved in a pain-free life.

9. Have you noticed any behavior or thought patterns that influence your perception of your pain? If you are busy or happy is your pain less? Do feelings of sadness increase your pain perception?

It is difficult to analyze your pain by yourself but you can if you put the effort into it. Use the chapter on self-analysis to work over your pain and its associations with your life and feelings. When you have some success, then go on to change these parts of your life.

Techniques

Now that you know and understand your pain complex better, here are some takeoff points for deprogramming your pain response. Try as many as you want and use those that work best. As you become more proficient, you will probably make up your own techniques. Just as an advanced guitar player can improvise after mastering the basics, so can you be creative in your approaches to health.

1. Induce hypnosis by focusing on the pain itself. Pay attention to it, see what it feels like, concentrate wholly on your pain and allow yourself to relax, paying attention to that sensation, whatever it is. See what it feels like as you focus your attention on it, notice how it waxes and wanes, increases and decreases. Note the quality, location, and intensity of your sensations. Using concentration, turn up your pain one click and see what that feels like. Notice that what was once uncomfortable is now just a sensation. Now turn it down two clicks. Wait and see what happens. Notice that you can predict when it will increase and decrease. You may want to repeat this technique numerous times, each time gaining mastery step by step. (Remember, small gains are important here.)

2. Under hypnosis, find your pain and visualize it as a fluffy white cloud floating in a blue sky. Pour your pain into that cloud and watch it float on the horizon, wafting in a gentle breeze. Allow the cloud to begin to dissipate, blow away. Watch as the cloud becomes wispy and tenuous. See how it floats slowly off, further and further away. Let your pain float off with the cloud, and allow your body to relax naturally and completely.

3. Under hypnosis, pinpoint the location of your pain and move it into another part of your body. If, for instance, you have lower back pain, move that pain into your left knee, allow your body to relax, noticing how, as the pain reaches your knee it becomes less and less, until you are left with only a slight discomfort in place of your low back pain.

4. Under hypnosis, visualize your pain control center. Close your eyes and find your pain center. See what comes into your mind as you ob-

serve what your pain control center looks like. Is it a series of switches, colored lights, thermostats, or knobs? Whatever it looks like, begin to learn to use those controls. Turn off the switches, dim the lights, continue to focus and concentrate as you turn up and down your subjective experience of pain. See yourself as the technician in charge of your pain control center.

5. Under hypnosis, change the sensation of pain into some other sensation. Realize that you can turn pain into a more comfortable sensation, perhaps a feeling of vibration, tingling, warmth, numbness, heaviness, fluidity. Many people learn to turn pain into pressure or numbness, replacing pain effectively with a different sensation.

6. Turn your pain into a color. A soothing peaceful color that is particularly meaningful to you.

7. Using visual imagery, picture your pain as a tightly wound rubber band. Then focus on the rubber band as it slowly unwinds, leaving you with a feeling of release. As the tension of the rubber band relaxes, you feel loose and pliable.

8. Under hypnosis, locate your pain and begin moving it down through your body, slowly, gradually, letting the pain flow out of your body and into the chair, the earth, the air.

9. Think about whatever relieves your pain the most. It might be a warm bath, a pill, being quiet in a dark room, or a brisk walk through the park. Since you have the memory of pain relief built into your mental computer, simply reproduce that experience and let it relieve your pain. Hook yourself into your memory bank and play back the tape that previously rid you of unwelcome pain. A quick technique here to

get you started is to remember your last shot of Novocain from the dentist. Reproduce that sensation in your jaw. For many people, this can be accomplished in a minute or two.

10. To convince yourself that you can control your pain, use hypnosis and concentrate on making a part of your body itch. Focus on the sensation of itching, and make it appear somewhere on your body, perhaps on your hand or foot. When you feel the itch and when it demands scratching, switch to another technique involving active fantasy. See yourself in a pleasant situation of your choosing. You will notice that you have "forgotten" the itch (you gain more control). You didn't have to scratch the itch you created, you forgot it (turned it off).

Case Histories

Case One

Sergeant F., a radar maintenance supervisor in the Air Force, was referred to me by a military neurologist who had treated the sergeant's headaches for about two years without success. These types of cases are often declared "medically refractory." Loosely translated, this means "nothing helps."

When I first saw him in the waiting room of the clinic, I observed a slightly overweight but immaculately uniformed master sergeant, who appeared resentful and somewhat impatient. His chest was covered with ribbons, and his shoes made mine look as if they had been polished with a Hershey bar. He came into my office and began by giving me a medical recital in a crisp no-nonsense style.

For eight years, Sergeant F. had been experiencing debilitating headaches at least three times a week. Recently, they had increased in frequency and strength. He was now taking addictive drugs and often had to go to the emergency room for injections to take the edge off his pain so he could sleep. At home, Sergeant F. had five or six types of medication that he was currently taking, plus a whole medicine cabinet full of pills that hadn't helped. An intense type of person who took great pride in his work, he was wondering if he would have to retire early from the service. He felt frustrated, hopeless, and not at all happy about being referred to a psychiatrist.

"I can see no reason for being here, sir," he told me sharply. "I guess they think I am crazy, but it is not all in my head."

As we talked, a plan for helping him began to emerge. I saw him as the kind of pragmatic, goal-oriented individual who likes to get things done. Help for this man would have to be done his way. We spent the entire first session discussing in detail his symptoms, personality, family, and social life. He repeated statements like, "They can't make me do this," and "Nobody can convince me otherwise." It developed that Sergeant F.'s family was suffering along with him. Mrs. F. got sympathetic headaches herself and saw her role as maintaining the family's emotional stability at whatever cost to herself. Their children had begun to tiptoe around the house in response to father's illness.

At the end of the first session, I introduced him to

the idea that a person's body is like a machine that can be tuned or repaired in more than one way. He looked skeptical, but agreed to return and explore the problem further. Hypnosis was discussed in mechanical terms, and he was given some literature about it.

The next time I saw him, we spent our time together drawing the human nervous system on a blackboard as an electrical diagram, using words that made sense to him like *circuits*, *resistors*, *capacitors*, and *switches*. Soon we had the entire blackboard covered with diagrams that only he and I could understand. At the end of the session I informed him that hypnosis would be used at our next meeting.

When he arrived the next week, he promptly sat down, propped his elbow on the desk, leaned his head against his fist and said, "Okay, go ahead and try, but you can't hypnotize me!"

This was a perfect situation for hypnosis since his attention was focused, his expectatons, although negative, were high, and his desires, although opposite to mine, were strong. I looked at him just as seriously and said, "You are right, no one can hypnotize you. No matter how hard I try, I can't hypnotize you. You won't relax. As a matter of fact, why don't you make your arm as stiff as iron and weld your fist to your head. Make your body rigid, and no matter how hard you try, you won't be able to relax."

At first, he looked startled and then he began to have a glazed, almost dazed appearance as his facial muscles began to relax and his eyes to close.

"Your arm is more and more like steel. It won't relax. Even though you could relax and help yourself, you probably won't be able to. So make your whole body tense and rigid. Even though you would like to make your body work for you, you probably won't be able to do so. Continue to get tighter and tighter."

By this time, he was in a medium trance. I continued to make suggestions that were couched in terms that reinforced his personality traits. Since he was a person who insisted on doing things his way, he was being given permission to help himself and to resist me at the same time. His bodily reactions were put in engineering-electronic terms, such as, "You could turn down your rheostat if you knew where it was, but you may not be able to."

When he came out of his trance and was fully alert again, he said, "I knew you wouldn't be able to hypnotize me. Nothing happened."

I asked him to begin keeping a pain log, and I also asked him to draw an electrical circuit diagram of his conception of his own body for our next meeting. In later sessions, we concentrated on learning the skills of what he called "relaxing," and he worked on picturing his body as a complicated electrical circuit system, with multiple on/off switches that he could control. He was also fascinated by the biofeedback machines in the clinic and enjoyed experimenting with them.

Four weeks later, at our last meeting, he spoke about changes in his pain symptoms, but made it quite clear that they had nothing to do with hypnosis, our clinic, or anything I had done. He said that he had gained control of his headaches, that he had done it his way, one which involved a complicated process of thinking through his own circuitry and turning off his head-aches at will. He rarely had headaches now, he told me, and only used Tylenol when he did.

"I know you tried real hard," he said sincerely. "Thanks a lot, Doc, but you know, you really have to do things yourself." I congratulated him on his break-through and he left triumphantly with a feeling of mastery. He thought that even though I had tried very hard, it was really he who had helped himself.

And, of course, he was right.

Case Two

Mrs. G., a twenty-nine-year-old mother of two, had been referred to me by her gynecologist. She was suffering from chronic pelvic pain of seven years' duration, a pain she described as "dull and aching." Her gynecologist felt her symptoms might be attributed to psychic causes. By this, he didn't mean it was all in her head.

Of course her pain was not in her head. It was in her pelvis, just as she said. She was not a liar nor a malingerer nor "bad and weak." As I read the consultation sheet about her many gynecological visits, tests, and procedures, the same old story surfaced. Here was a woman in pain, yet she had not received any help from medical intervention.

In all her attempts at getting help for her pain, I suspected that an important aspect had been consistently overlooked. That aspect was her psychological construction and how it might be working against her rather than with her. She hadn't learned to gain mastery over her symptoms, much less her body. Medical professionals sometimes tend to treat the human body as a machine that needs fixing rather than as a dynamic organism that can alter its own state.

Mrs. G., when she came into my office, was apprehensive and not overjoyed to be there. She was neatly and conservatively dressed and sat erect in the chair with her ankles crossed and her handbag held securely in her lap. When I asked her how I could help her, she responded, "I'm not sure. Dr. B. wanted me to come here since we are considering surgery. I have been scheduled for a hysterectomy next month."

I knew that her gynecologist felt that before such a drastic step as surgery, psychiatric consultation was in order for Mrs. G. He had written on her consultation sheet, "Tense and uptight woman; request evaluation for surgery."

Before we discussed her pain, Mrs. G. gave me an "organ recital" of her past history with pelvic pain. Her trouble began seven years ago and was at first intermittent. But now, she said, pain was a part of her daily life. Four years ago she had a laparoscopy, the insertion of a periscope-like device through an incision in the anterior abdominal wall; it revealed nothing wrong. Three months ago, she underwent an exploratory laparotomy, at which time some minor adhesions of her uterus and right fallopian tube were seen and corrected. But nothing was found that explained her pelvic pain and dysphoria. It was hoped that the surgical removal of her reproductive organs would end the pain.

"How do you feel about having a hysterectomy?" I asked her.

"Well, I am not wild about the idea, but I would do anything to end the pain."

"Let us talk about your pain. Tell me what it is like for you."

Again, she described the dull aching that she experienced chronically in her pelvis. I asked her to draw a diagram of her day in relation to her pain, and she went to the blackboard to explain her routine. The pain began as soon as she got up in the morning and continued through her morning chores, easing up only after lunch, when she was able to lie down.

"Is the pain worse when you are up and around?" I asked.

"Sometimes, but other times, when I am really busy, I don't notice it as much. I have to force myself to do most things, but once I am working, the pain doesn't seem as bad."

"So one way you fight pain is by keeping busy. Anything else that you have noticed that helps?"

"A warm bath. Sometimes at night when the kids are in bed and my husband is watching TV, I take a long hot bath and that is nice."

"What about sleeping? Does the pain bother you then?"

"Lots of times I take a pill. Some days I take as many as four or five when the pain is really bad. Even then, I often have trouble falling asleep."

"How do you feel about the pain itself?"

"I hate it, naturally. And I hate burdening my husband and children with it. It isn't fair to make them suffer for my pain.''

"I can see you are a person who likes to do things for herself. The pain is limiting your independence, isn't it?''

"Exactly! I don't like to take those pills, either.''

"I think I can help you learn to be more in control of your pain. Through self-hypnosis, you can learn to interrupt your pain cycle and give yourself relief from pain. Are you interested?''

She was, and we discussed hypnosis and keeping a pain log. Since her surgery was scheduled so soon, we agreed to work together intensively to see if it would be possible for her to gain control over her pain and avoid undergoing the hysterectomy.

At our next session, later that week, Mrs. G. achieved a mild trance through eye fixation and progressive muscular relaxation. She reported that the concentration and resulting relaxation eased the ache in her pelvis slightly, and she was excited about learning a new skill that she felt had great possibilities for her particular condition.

The next time we met, she told me she had been practicing five or six times a day while sitting in a chair in her living room and staring at a corner of the ceiling, concentrating on relaxing each muscle of her body. She showed me how she was doing this. When she was in a medium trance, I suggested that she focus on her pelvis and concentrate on creating the sensation of pain. As she did this, I noticed how her eyes flickered beneath her closed lids, a good sign of hypnosis. When she announced that the pain was there, I said,

"Now that you have seen how you can make the pain arrive, how you can control the sensations in your pelvis, try letting the pain recede again, letting your pelvis relax again, feeling those warm waves of pleasant relaxation sweep over your whole abdominal area." She was able to do this. When she came out of her trance we discussed the importance of what had just happened.

She continued to practice at home, and at our next session we induced hypnosis through the active fantasy of relaxing in a warm bath. The pain went away, she told me, as soon as she saw herself sinking into the warm water, and she was anxious to go home and see if she could induce the same feelings away from my office.

That afternoon, she called me and told me she had just spoken to her gynecologist and cancelled her appointment for surgery. She sounded confident and happy and told me she was looking forward to our next session. More about that session follows in the next chapter.

Case Three

Mr. W., a thirty-two-year-old police officer, was referred to me by his general practitioner, who hoped that some type of relaxation therapy might help Mr. W.'s lower back spasms. Both the patient and his physician were also worried about Mr. W.'s growing dependence on the pain medication he was taking: Fiorinal, Valium and alcohol.

When I met him, Mr. W., a neatly dressed, obviously tense man, appeared angry. "I don't know why my doctor wanted me to see you," he announced. "My problem is back pain."

We discussed his symptoms, which included a five-year history of lower back pain that began with a muscle sprain. Disc disease (herniated intervertebral disc syndrome) was suspected because his pain was worse when he lifted heavy objects, but there was no organic sign of injury.

Mr. W.'s rigid posture emphasized his polite but distant attitude. "I think my doctor has just about given up on me," he said. "Since he can't find the cause of my pain, he has sent me to a psychiatrist! Maybe he thinks I am imagining it."

I reassured Mr. W. that I thought his pain was real. It was in his back, I knew, not his head. "In this clinic," I explained, "we teach people to manage their pain. I know you are not here for psychotherapy."

He seemed relieved and somewhat mollified, so I went on. "Often stress is related to the kind of muscle spasms you seem to be having. Perhaps you injured your back in the past and your muscles tightened up. An example of how that happens is the way a dog deals with a fractured leg, pulling it up close to his body and stiffening the leg, which gives the leg a chance to heal. It is a generalized fact of nature that injury leads to muscle stiffness that protects the injured area. So if you injured your back sometime in the past, the huge muscle groups along your back may tighten up and become spastic and rigid. You can get into cycles of recurrent spasms, pain, more spasm, and continued pain. Muscle relaxants like Valium try to interrupt this cycle but, in your case, this isn't happening.''

Mr. W. understood and agreed. "So if this is the case," he asked, "what can I do about it?"

"Often the resulting spasm, though at first useful, can get out of control and become the source of the pain itself. By affecting the level of spasm or even learning to decrease the pain directly, you can break the pain cycle."

Mr. W. agreed to keep a pain log. I explained that each hour of the day he should note the quality of pain on a scale from one to ten, the location and type (aching, gripping, burning, etc.) of pain, any associated activities or emotional states (helplessness, anxiety, boredom, etc.), and whatever method he used to take care of the pain (endure it, take a pill, hot tub, etc.).

The next week he returned enthusiastic and reported his findings. His back pain didn't begin until mid-morning, he told me, continued through his work day, and eased up usually around five or six o'clock. Then, it returned around nine or ten at night, just before he went to bed. He got the most relief, he said, by putting a heating pad on his back while he watched TV and drank a beer after work. He was unable to explain the end of the day recurrence of not only pain but spasm.

I asked him to describe a typical work day in terms of his pain, and he told me that the pain didn't usually begin until after he had taken care of the most pressing business. It started when he had had his third or fourth cup of coffee and began looking at the less urgent business. At least 80 percent of his work day, he told me, was spent at his desk, and he casually mentioned that,

"I don't think my back hurt me nearly as much when I was more active."

"Oh? When was that?"

"I used to have a regular police beat, vice squad, until I was promoted to a desk job. Since then, my back has hurt a lot worse. Do you think all the added responsibility and being at a desk all day has anything to do with it?"

"Sounds pretty logical to me."

"Still," he continued, "why does the pain go away in the late afternoon and then come back late at night?"

We went over his day again, and he mentioned that it was his habit to get out his briefcase before going to bed, using that time to prepare for the next day's work. Therefore, we decided, his late night pain was probably an anticipatory response to the pressure of his job.

Realizing that work-related things tended to increase his pain and that anything that took his mind away from work seemed to decrease it, we searched for a hypnotic technique that would make use of this. A weekend jogger, Mr. W. spoke openly of the enjoyment he found in running and especially the feeling of looseness in his back and legs that he experienced while jogging. He always ran in the early morning, finding the streets quiet and the air invigorating.

We induced hypnosis by progressive muscular relaxation, even though Mr. W. was unable to relax the large muscles in his back. We skipped over those after he had relaxed them as much as possible, and from there we concentrated on the active fantasy of jogging, re-creating the emotional mind-set he enjoyed while running. Mr. W. learned to master these techniques after two more sessions and reported that he was finding increasing relief for his back pain. He was able to practice self-hypnosis several times a day, both at work and at home.

When he called me six weeks later with a follow-up report, he told me that he was having some success using the key word or stimulus technique, inducing hypnosis rapidly by projecting a mental image of himself jogging silently through the city dawn. His back muscles were relaxing and the spasms had almost ceased. He spoke with confidence and told me his back wasn't hurting him at all as we talked. That was two o'clock in the afternoon!

8. Improving Your Sex Life

When asked, "What is normal?" Sigmund Freud replied, "The ability to work, to play, and to love."

The possibility of sharing true intimacy, which is humankind's highest achievement, can become a reality through self-hypnosis. For those lucky people who already have a satisfying sex life, self-hypnosis can be used to enhance that pleasure for both partners. Once you have learned the techniques for hypnotic relaxation, innovation becomes the key which can allow you to express yourself sexually in new and different ways.

The following is designed to help you improve your sex life. It can be used as a general guideline for developing your own needs or desires.

Self-Analysis

Take several sessions of self-hypnosis to reexamine
and rethink your sexuality, with the intention of learning more about yourself and your sexuality as your
goal. Here are some questions you can ponder when,
under hypnosis, you feel receptive to exploring your
feelings about sex.

1. When did you have your first sexual experience?
   What was it like?

2. Think about your parents' attitudes toward sex.
   Look back and reexamine what they told you,
   both in words and by their behavior. How did
   you feel about it then? How do you feel now?

3. Think about your sexual experiences with other
   people. When did they begin and how have they
   changed? How important is love, closeness, intimacy, warmth, and bonding to your ability to
   express yourself sexually?

4. Let your thoughts dwell on your body and its
   sexuality. How were you allowed to feel about
   your body as a child? Was it yours to love and
   take care of? How did you feel when it began
   to change in puberty? How do you feel about it
   now? Has age, childbirth, obesity, or surgery
   changed your feelings about your body's sexuality?

5. Has the bedroom become a battleground? Do
   you use your sexual favors as trading stamps to
   gain nonsexual concessions from your partner?
   Is sex a silent struggle? How do anger, hostility,
   and guilt enter into your sex life?

6. Has sex become routine for you?

7. What sex habits have you developed over the years? Do you require darkness or a romantic atmosphere? What kinds of fantasies are stimulating for you? How would you like to change your sex habits now?

Practice relaxing and enjoying your new sexual desires and attitudes. Practice relaxing during intercourse and see what it is like. You will be more able to prolong, enjoy, and control your sexual life as you relax.

Three Case Studies

Self-Hypnosis and Orgasm

Mrs. G., already encountered in the preceding chapter, had been suffering chronic pelvic pain for seven years. After learning the techniques of self-hypnosis, she was able to begin to control her pain, making it come and go at will. After a few sessions, when she had reported considerable success in her pain control, she ended one of her joyous descriptions of her new, pain-lessened life with these words: "Now that my pain is better, doctor, I feel as if there is something missing in my life."

"What do you mean?" I asked.

"Well, my enjoyment of sex leaves something to be desired."

"How do you enjoy it? I gather not much."

"I can take it or leave it, really."

"Has it always been this way?"

"Well," she said, blushing and fidgeting with her purse, "there was a man I was engaged to once, and I enjoyed it with him."

"Did you have orgasms?"

"I think maybe I did. Of course, we never went to bed together, you understand, just some heavy petting and so forth. Then he went to Vietnam and was killed there. Later, I met my husband, but I've never recaptured that exciting feeling. Even our honeymoon was terrible. I was exhausted and having postmenstrual cramps. I tried to keep from him the fact that I wasn't enjoying it. But there have been times in our married life that sex has been pleasant."

"Do you have orgasms now?"

"I don't know. Maybe, but I don't think so."

When I asked Mrs. G. to describe what her feelings were when she and her husband made love, she described them as warm and pleasant, but mentioned that intercourse was over too fast or the pain began before she could really enjoy it. Her husband, she was quick to point out, was considerate and loving and spent a lot of time in foreplay, but, although she liked being held and hugged and kissed, she found the mechanics of sex more of a chore than a pleasure. She denied feeling angry about her sex life, but used the word *resent* when she talked about all that she had read and seen on TV about sex. She felt she was missing something important that other people were enjoying.

"What about masturbation?" I asked. "What technique do you use?"

"Why, I don't masturbate," she replied. "I'm married! And anyway, masturbation isn't nice."

When I asked her why she thought this, her response was vehement. She remembered an incident from her childhood when her mother had come into her room and found her playing with a doll under the sheets. Although Mrs. G. does not think she was masturbating then, she vividly remembers her mother's anger. It developed that her parents were prudish about sex and never showed any affection, sexual or otherwise, to each other in front of their children.

"So," I said, "perhaps you still think of masturbation as forbidden?"

"But I'm married," she continued to protest.

"Still, I have a feeling there is something missing in your life," I said, repeating back her own words.

"Yes, I'm beginning to think so."

I took this opportunity to emphasize the positive aspects of sex, how it can be humankind's most fulfilling experience, the sharing of true intimacy, and a way for us, as adults, to play.

"Would it be worthwhile," I asked her, "to rethink your attitude about sex under self-hypnosis? You might want to explore your parents' attitudes and think about how you are a grown woman now, and it is no longer appropriate for you to feel guilty about a healthy sex life. Do you think you could give yourself permission to relax and enjoy your sexuality?"

"I suppose I ought to try to do that," she replied.

"While you are asking yourself those things, I'd like you to be aware of how often you use words like *should* and *ought*. These are words of parental injunction that can still undermine our own free choice."

When I saw her next, she reported that she had discovered that "should" and "ought" prefaced many of her thoughts about sex. Sex, she realized, was something her mother had taught her was dirty. Under self-hypnosis she remembered an incident at a party about four years ago. Her mother had advised her not to drink any more wine. "Be careful," she had admonished her daughter, "something might happen." Under self-hypnosis, Mrs. G. not only remembered the buried incident but also remembered that she had indeed quit drinking wine that night, feeling bad about the possibility of being "seduced" by her husband, as if it might be something nasty.

At our next session, we discussed ways Mrs. G. might use self-hypnosis to loosen herself up for sex. She rejected masturbation since she was sure she would feel too guilty. So I suggested that she use self-hypnosis like a glass of wine before bed to help her look forward with happy expectation to intercourse with her husband in the free, happy mood of a mature adult. Then, taking my cue from the information she had already given me about how a hot tub had occasionally relieved her pelvic pain, I suggested that she plan a session of self-hypnosis in a warm bath before intercourse. At that time, I offered, she could relax completely and think pleasantly ahead to a rewarding sexual experience. She might want to focus on fantasies or past good sexual experiences, and she would want to concentrate her attention on her pelvis and the feelings of building sexual stimulation.

Two weeks later, she reported that she had success in improving her sex life, especially after the night she used self-hypnosis to help her relax. "But, Doctor," she told me, "it's strange, but as soon as I started to enjoy sex, the pain came back."

"Isn't it amazing," I asked her, "how your body makes the connection between pain and pleasure? It is important to notice when the pain comes and when it interferes with your enjoyment of sex. Have you given yourself permission to enjoy sex? Maybe you should try practicing that some more."

She did, and several weeks later she called. "My husband and I had a beautiful sexual experience last weekend," she told me. "We went away by ourselves, and I had an orgasm both nights! The pain seems to come and go with intercourse, but I have more control over it. But the best part of all this, I think, is that I am not snapping at the kids much any more. My daughter said to me yesterday, 'Mommy, you don't yell as much as you used to,' and I nearly cried, I was so happy!"

With Mrs. G., as with many people, enjoyment of sex was affected by many things:

1. Her current life situation.
2. Her past training about sex.
3. Her body.
4. Her psychological make-up.

Once she was able to control just a few of those variables, she found it easier to accept herself as a normal, healthy, sexually mature adult. The most important change she made was giving herself permission to be pain-free and sexually active, something that had previously been difficult for her because of the negative messages she was receiving from the memory bank in her mind.

Self-Hypnosis and the Impotent Man

I wasn't exactly sure what Mr. H.'s problem would turn out to be, since, on the form he filled out in my office, he answered the question, "For what problem are you seeking help?" by writing simply "marital problem."

Mr. H. was forty-three years old, the vice president of a large engineering concern. Yet, when I met him, he looked at the floor as we shook hands, his whole demeanor sad and glum. Right away he told me that he had been impotent for the last two weeks, a situation that was particularly distressing to him since he had been married only a few months. A widower with three teen-aged children, he explained that his first wife had died two years ago.

"I never had this problem before," he said with anguish. "When I was single I was able to have successful sexual relations with no problem. I tended to date much younger women until I met my new wife. She is everything I want in a mate, and that is why I can't understand this difficulty! I hope you can help me."

"It has been going on for two weeks?" I asked.

"Well, I haven't been able to get an erection for two weeks. Before that, my ability varied. Sometimes I could and sometimes not. It got steadily worse."

"And how have your children reacted to your new wife?"

"That's a problem, too. Naturally they resent what they see as her taking their mother's place. But it is something I am sure will work out with time. It is getting better already, actually."

After ascertaining that his impotence was not an indication of a chronic medical problem, and that he had been seen by his regular physician, he told me that his G.P.'s advice had been to forget about it and try to relax.

"I tried to do that," he explained, "but it persists. My wife is very understanding, but I am frightened about not feeling like a man. I wonder if it is all in my mind."

It seemed probable to me that Mr. H.'s difficulty stemmed from the fact that he was still grieving for his dead wife and felt guilty and unfaithful. His children's reluctance to accept his new wife added to it, but was really a minor point. Fortunately, Mr. H. had a great deal of self-awareness and saw readily the scope of his problem. His new wife, unlike the younger women with whom he had had sex in his bachelor days, shared many of the characteristics he had loved in his first wife.

We spent some time talking about grief and guilt, and then I explained the principles of self-hypnosis to him. He agreed it might help him. A moderate state of hypnosis was induced by having him concentrate on his left hand and wrist, noticing especially how his watchband felt where it touched his wrist. Then I asked him to concentrate on the index finger of his left hand and to allow himself to make that finger hypersensitive. As he noticed the change in feeling of his finger and left hand, I suggested that he would notice how his body was deeply relaxed, as can naturally happen when you focus on a specific body part (see chapter 3, Hypnotic Techniques). Then I told him that, although he was in a moderate trance, he would retain the ability to talk.

When he was completely relaxed, I suggested that he concentrate on the feelings he had experienced recently in his penis. When he had done this, he discovered that whenever he wanted to make love to his wife, his penis felt almost numb, empty, and drained. After he explored those feelings, which he associated with depression, I asked him to think about how his penis used to feel, when he was able to maintain an erection, and to concentrate on his pelvis and all the sensations it was capable of feeling. "Allow those feelings to return," I suggested, "and make your penis hypersensitive. Focus on the exquisite building of excitement in the shaft of your penis, and your entire pelvis. As a matter of fact," I told him, "it's now so sensitive that it feels like a gun about to go off. Ejaculation is so imminent that you might not be able to control it."

Since Mr. H. had rejected the idea of using self-hypnosis for self-analysis and was obviously a chronic worrier, I decided to suggest this scenario to him with the expectation that he would understand that he had substituted the worry about impotence for his worries about guilt and disloyalty. I knew, in order to focus on that worry, he must first get an erection. Once the hypnotic conditions were set up in this way, he could forget his impotence and direct his concern to premature ejaculation. (This technique can be reversed to help the problem of premature ejaculation. Instead of focusing on hypersensitivity of the penis, the person can concentrate on inducing numbness.)

The next week, Mr. H. appeared more self-assured. "It worked, Doc," he said happily, looking me in the eye. "I came before she did, but we finished up manually."

"That is fine," I answered. "And now you know that, through self-hypnosis, you can turn your sexual sensations up and down. Keep practicing. Now that your potency is so strong, you can learn to prolong your enjoyment by concentrating on other nonsexual experiences to delay ejaculation. Think about camping, for instance, to turn down the sensitivity. Some men will do math problems in their heads to control the excitement, and so last longer."

Mr. H., after he had realized and confronted his grief and guilt, was able to use self-hypnosis successfully to combat his temporary impotence. When that was over, he used it to prolong his own and his wife's enjoyment of sex.

At a six-month follow-up, he reported that these improvements continued. He related that he was using self-hypnosis infrequently, however, approximately once a month and this was usually only to relieve insomnia. He was invited to call me anytime in the future to talk about positive developments as well as to discuss any problems.

Self-Hypnosis and Improving an Already Satisfying Sex Life

I wish I had more patients like Mr. R., a twenty-eight-year-old bachelor who came to me simply because he wanted to improve his sex life.

"I have a very active sex life, Doctor," he said to me with an embarrassed grin. "But, lately, a couple of my sex partners have accused me of wanting only to add another notch to my gun, so to speak. And I don't like to think of myself that way. Sex is terrific, but sometimes it does seem a bit mechanical. Can you help me with that?"

As we talked, I saw that he was one of those fortunate people who have a healthy, well-developed sexuality and sensuality. The comments of his sex partners had hurt him because he genuinely viewed sex as a warm, sharing experience, one that should be equally meaningful to both participants. We talked about his hobbies and interests, and it developed that he was an avid skier.

"Skiing is a real turn-on," he said, "and, since I am good at it, I can relax and enjoy everything about it. I like the whole scene—the snow and the feel of the wind on my face, as well as the ski lodge and sitting before the fire with good friends."

We took off from there, and, when I had explained the principles of self-hypnosis, we decided that he could use it to re-create the same skiing images while he was enjoying sex with a partner. He could concentrate on the sensations in his pelvis as he skied downhill in hypnotic fantasy. He could remember the sense of flying before the wind, racing down the mountain. Or he could think about the slower, meandering side-to-side movement of a more leisurely descent. Just as he could control his movements on skis, he could control his sexual excitement, and so pace the experience to the rate that was most appealing to himself and his partner.

The image of the ski lodge was a good one for re-creating the atmosphere of warmth and shared intimacy that was important to him. He suggested to himself that he would concentrate on seeing himself and his partner before a crackling fire in the ski lodge, sitting close together and talking and listening carefully to each other. He wanted to re-create that sense of being close and loving and apply it to the loving closeness he wanted to feel in sex. Through self-hypnosis, Mr. R. was able to add a new dimension to his sexuality and work on erasing the mechanical aspects of his sex life that had caused his concern.

Conclusion

Like hunger, sex is one of humankind's strongest urges. To be unable to fully enjoy your sexuality can be a severe loss. Self-hypnosis is one tool for gaining a better understanding of what it means to be a sexually mature adult. Through self-analysis, you can explore your sexual past and your present feelings and make decisions about how you want the future to be. Self-hypnosis can help you relax enough to enjoy the experience of getting to know your own sexual needs and pleasures. Partnership sex can be enhanced and enriched through the insights gained in self-analysis. Hypnotic techniques can be practiced to allow yourself and your partner to reach new heights of sexual gratification.

Self-hypnosis can also be constructive in dealing with sexual dysfunctions, such as impotence, premature ejaculation, sexual incompatibility, lack of orgasm and dyspareunia (discomfort during intercourse).

9. Hypnosis Yesterday and Today

Hypnosis has always been difficult to discuss rationally, to investigate, even to think about in a logical manner. Incomprehensible to most people, it has often eluded scientific description. Variously described as magic, an act of the gods, religious experience, possession by demons, mental illness, charlatanism, trance, state of supersuggestibility, simple cooperation, surrendering of a weak will to a stronger one, fluid emanating from a person's body, and animal magnetism, it has also been declared not to exist at all.

The definition of hypnosis I follow is: An altered state of consciousness attainable by almost anyone, a state of (1) increased concentration, (2) distraction from ordinary thinking processes, and (3) cooperation either with oneself or another. These three elements of hypnosis are recognizable in many human experiences, including studying, daydreaming, and commuting. Apparently, the ability to alter one's state of consciousness, whether it is called hypnosis or something else, is often practiced.

Why, then, has hypnosis had such a stormy course through history? Why do large segments of both the lay public and the scientific community view it with suspicion or disdain? Some of the reasons for the oftentimes shady reputation of hypnosis may be the poor company it has historically kept.

Charlatans and con men have used hypnoticlike phenomena to delude their victims with the lure of money or get-rich-quick schemes. Many early hypnotic experimenters, like Anton Mesmer, Viennese physician of our Revolutionary War era (from whom the word *mesmerism* derives) took advantage of the intense emotional reactions to hypnosis to make sizable fortunes. The ability to induce a hypnoticlike state is often part of the charisma of a powerful leader, whose followers are too often blinded by the aura of power, sometimes to the point of "mass hysteria."

The fortune teller, with hands waving slowly over a crystal ball, uses hypnotic elements to take advantage of a client's desire to learn the future. Stage hypnotists often choreograph dramatic and unusual events in which they seem to control others. Hypnosis is associated with sexual seduction; the Svengali myth caters to the image of a helpless but beautiful maiden who falls under the evil influence of a powerful hypnotist.

The common denominator of these sketches is, of course, the association of hypnosis with evil, as if hypnosis were a secret skill used to corrupt innocent victims. Understanding this, it's no wonder some people view the process with anxious trepidation.

This chapter will provide an outline of the history of hypnosis, explain how hypnotic phenomena have come to be connected with shady events in the past, and describe the bumpy road hypnosis has travelled to attain wide acceptance today.

Hypnosis in the Distant Past

Hypnosis has probably been with us as long as we have been human. Anthropologists and archeologists have documented cases of primitive civilizations using hypnotic phenomena to cure illness, bring tribes to a state of frenzy in times of impending warfare, and to augment religious ecstasy during celebrations and fertility rites.

Most primitive tribes counted among their members a shaman, medicine man, or wise woman, who was responsible for diagnosing illness, interceding with the gods, and acting as an intermediary between this world and the spirit world. These physicians made use of hypnotic processes, channeling natural human brain power to achieve desired goals. When their efforts worked, they assumed credit; when they didn't work, they suffered the blame. It was a risky business.

Archeologists have unearthed evidence of "sleep temples" in ancient Egypt, havens of tranquility where suffering humans brought their physical and emotional troubles to be cured. The patient entered the healing temple and was counselled and instructed by the priest-

or priestess-physician to sleep and dream within the confines of the temple. When this was accomplished, the dreams were interpreted and appropriate herbs, drugs, or rites were prescribed to effect a cure.

There are also many recorded instances of hypnotic phenomena in biblical times. The Old Testament recounts how "the Lord God caused a deep sleep to fall upon Adam" (Genesis 2:21-22). The New Testament chronicles how Jesus used his charisma to heal the sick with a touch or cast out demons. This can be seen as a parallel to the technique discussed in the chapter on pain, where pain can be moved out of one's body and dispersed into the ground or the air or another part of the body.

One of the best examples of hypnotic phenomena can be found in certain American Indian rituals of entry into manhood. The man-to-be had many tasks to perform before being welcomed into the tribe as a man, but often these tasks included a period of isolation from other people in search of a vision. When the vision came, it usually appeared in the form of a dream or hypnagogic phenomenon, which is a state of fatigue akin to sleep. The necessary elements for hypnosis were undoubtedly present in the young Indian: high expectations, distractibility (by isolation), concentration (focusing on awakening his vision), and cooperation (with the Great Spirit or other supernatural being). When the dream or vision occurred, the young man returned to the tribe to have the medicine man interpret what he had experienced. Whatever it was, it had deep personal significance for him the rest of his life and often evolved into the worship of a totem all his own.

Hypnosis probably showed up in many civilizations as a way of passing on a unique culture. The rituals of memorizing the sevenfold ways of Buddha in India involved long hours of sitting still and contemplating ideas, thoughts, or objects—all of which are essential elements of hypnosis. In early Hawaiian history, as well as in many other cultures, young people learned their history and genealogy through hypnotic rituals of rhythmic chanting and memorization.

Many Eastern forms of mind and body control use the elements of hypnosis. Karate, judo, jujitsu, and Tai Chi are only some of the disciplines which employ concentration, distraction, meditation, and cooperation to achieve desired results. No one who has seen a demonstration of karate, for example, and watched a bare-handed man break boards and bricks can doubt that extreme mental control and physiological obedience, when combined, can have astonishing results.

Who's Who in Medical Hypnosis

Anton Mesmer (1734-1815)

Mesmer was the first person in modern times to devise a standard system of inducing trance. He called his system "animal magnetism" and postulated that its force had something to do with the movement of the sun, planets, and stars. This force was passed into the subject by way of magnets. Legend has it that Mesmer first obtained his "magnets" from a Jesuit priest named Father Maximilian Hell.

As Mesmer experimented with inducing trance by rubbing magnets over the bodies of afflicted persons, he noticed unusual behavior, often leading to convulsions, which he called "crises." People flocked to him for help, and he became very rich. As demand for his treatments grew, he began to treat people in groups, or séances. Mesmer arranged his groups with the skill of a modern choreographer, sprinkling each séance with a number of attractive young men and women. He had his subjects sit in a darkened room, lighted only by flickering candles around a tub filled with water and iron filings. Iron rods protruded from the tub, called a *baquet*. As his assistants prepared the group for the arrival of the master, excitement and high anticipation reigned. At the precise moment of highest expectation, Mesmer would enter the room dramatically, often dressed in flowing robes of purple. When the séance began, Mesmer would go from person to person, touching and stroking them. The "crisis" or convulsions often experienced by Mesmer's subjects were sensual in nature. Sometimes people would roll on the floor, talk in tongues, and go through periods of apparent ecstasy.

A commission formed to investigate Mesmer's activities in France (which included among its members the American ambassador to France, Benjamin Franklin) described the process: "The experimenter . . . passes his right hand behind the woman's body and they incline toward each other so as to favor this twofold contact. This causes the closest proximity. The two faces almost touch. The breath is intermingled. All physical impressions are felt in common and a reciprocal attraction of sexes must constantly be excited in all its force.'' As a result of the commission's findings, Mesmer was declared a fraud and driven from France. He died a pauper in Vienna.

Armand, Marquis de Puysegur (1757-1828)

A man of unquestioned reputation and a former student of Mesmer, Puysegur continued exploring the induction of trance. He had many erroneous assumptions about hypnosis, but did discover several facts. One was the marked influence on trance by the interaction between the hypnotist and the subject; another was the discovery of the ''waking trance,'' where subjects can talk and carry on other activities while in a state of hypnosis.

James Braid (1795-1860)

James Braid, Scottish physician and surgeon, became interested in the medical aspects of hypnosis. He devised the technique of eye fixation, and coined the term ''neurohypnosis'' (from Hypnos, the Greek god of sleep) for what had formerly been termed ''animal magnetism.''

James Esdaile (1808-1895)

Another Scottish surgeon, Dr. Esdaile served a tour of duty in India, where he performed over three hundred operations using hypnosis as anesthesia. Surviving reports detail the massive nature of most of the operations he performed on native Indians, including surgical removal of tumors. Mortality rates for similar operations at that time were as high as 50 percent, while Esdaile's reported mortality rate for operations done under hypnosis averaged only 5 percent. The introduction around this time of chloroform as an anesthetic led to a decline in interest in "Mesmerism" as anesthesia.

Jean-Martin Charcot (1825-1893)

French psychiatrist, professor of pathology and probably the most famous neurologist of his time, Dr. Charcot used hypnosis extensively to treat a wide variety of medical complaints. He believed, however, that entrance into a hypnotic state was prima facie evidence of a hysterical personality and thought that a person had to be mentally ill in order to be hypnotized. Many distinguished scientists and physicians came to Paris to study under Charcot, including Sigmund Freud.

A. Liebeault (1823-1904)

A rural French physician, Dr. Liebeault practiced hypnosis unheralded for twenty years. Although rejected and deemed a fraud by the medical profession at large, Dr. Liebeault was widely acclaimed by his patients.

Hippolyte Bernheim (1840-1919)

Dr. Bernheim, a famous French psychotherapist, observed the work of Liebeault. Together, they founded the Nancy School (named for the city of Nancy in France), which had considerable influence on French psychiatry for a great number of years. Once again, hypnosis became a reputable mode of treatment, and many physicians came to Nancy to study and attempt to discover the "secret of hypnosis" for their own practice.

Sigmund Freud (1856-1939)

Freud, unquestionably the most well-known psychiatrist to date, studied hypnosis under Charcot. With his insatiable curiosity about human mental processes, Freud, also a neurologist, used hypnosis to achieve cures which seemed miraculous to him. Gradually, however, he became disenchanted with hypnosis as a sole means of treatment because he felt that the cures achieved were often only temporary and that not everyone was capable of entering a trance. He felt foolish when he was unable to induce it, and, finally, he was unable to explain much of the material patients presented to him under hypnosis.

In a now famous case, Freud collaborated with a fellow neurologist, Josef Breuer (1842-1925), who had developed what he called "the talking cure" to help his patient, Anna O., with her hysterical attacks. From his association with Breuer and his patient, Freud began to use this method, both with and without hypnosis, and gradually the method of free association evolved. Before abandoning the practice of hypnosis (some believe because he found it "too seductive"), Freud used it in therapy and discovered the mechanism of repression of unwelcome impulses, and that catharsis of these thoughts brought at least temporary improvement of a number of conditions. Freud's eventual repudiation of hypnosis for medical treatment led to its discredit, and hypnosis was once again relegated to charlatans and stage shows.

Hypnosis Today

In more modern times, researchers have turned again to hypnosis as a powerful tool for helping humankind understand itself. In 1955, the British Medical Association formally endorsed the teaching of hypnosis in medical schools and approved it as a recognized form of medical practice. In 1958, the American Psychological Association formed a specialty in hypnosis and established a certifying board of examiners in both clinical and experimental hypnosis.

Today, hypnosis is approved as a legitimate medical practice by the American Medical Association, and there are at least two prominent American societies that deal mainly with research and treatment methods in hypnosis. Currently, in the United States, scientific professionals use hypnosis in both clinical and experimental settings. Continuing research provides extensive data, and the interested reader will find a wide variety of material in scientific journals, published books, and media coverage. Hypnosis is once again enjoying a period of respectability and is viewed with serious interest by both scientific professionals and the general public.

Stage Hypnosis

People are fascinated by hypnosis and entertainers take advantage of that fascination to use the more bizarre aspects of behavior under hypnosis to give the public a run for their money.

The stage hypnotist usually has a good idea of what the audience wants and works hard to give it to them. Many stage hypnotists dress the part, often wearing black robes lined in scarlet satin. Often an attractive woman, scantily clad, assists. First, the hypnotist-entertainer sizes up the audience while delivering a general explanation of the "mysteries" of hypnosis. When audience expectations and interest are sufficiently whetted, the stage hypnotist may demonstrate an induction technique, asking all spectators to participate. An induction technique such as hand clasping is most often the one picked because it affords the stage hypnotist the opportunity to select volunteers from among those who cannot unclasp their hands until they are given specific permission.

Checking out the manner in which potential subjects indicate their willingness to volunteer is another way the hypnotist-entertainer chooses subjects. For instance, a person whose head nods rhythmically in agreement with the carefully toned suggestion for volunteers to make themselves known will be among the first chosen. At the same time, the person who laughs and jabs a neighbor with an elbow while volunteering will probably not be picked. In any audience, 5 to 10 percent will prove to be excellent hypnotic subjects, capable of a deep trance. The stage hypnotist knows how to recognize them using these techniques.

Again, even a stage hypnotist cannot force a subject to behave contrary to his or her moral beliefs. The amusing and unusual antics people display on stage are usually the result of group expectation coupled with the other aspects of appearing before a live audience.

Hypnosis and the Occult

Literary descriptions of the rites of witchcraft contain many hypnotic elements, including chants and rituals, focusing of attention on wavering candles and various totems, and an atmosphere of highly charged group expectations. Many people go to fortune-tellers and other spiritualists with high expectations, and some are in a hypnoticlike trance the moment they enter the curtained alcoves where the fortune-teller reads the tea leaves or the crystal ball.

The association of hypnosis with the occult is well documented but tenuous, and there are, of course, many other factors at work when people dabble in the occult. But some of the phenomena associated with occultism are definitely hypnotic and can be explained in hypnotic terms.

Water-witching, or divining, is one example. The V-shaped branch used by the water-witcher to find water sources is, first of all, intrinsically unstable because of the way it has to be held in the hands and therefore tends to point downward. But, possibly the most important reason why water-witchers succeed in finding water can be attributed to their unconscious computer that tells them where the most likely site for water is. There are many clues in a landscape that indicate where water will be found, including the color, type, and distribution of vegetation and the types of rock formations and soil. There are other clues as well, most too subtle to be consciously noted. By holding the divining rod in the appropriate way, the witcher's ideomotor movements (small body movements that are unconscious) will point the stick at the correct spot.

A good witcher is often 70 to 80 percent correct in finding a good spot for a well, but it is not magic. It is simply a question of knowing the territory. Water-witching is often an "inherited" ability. Offspring learn it at their parents' sides, learning the technique while unconsciously learning to recognize the particular land areas where water is likely to be found. This conscious and unconscious learned material finds expression through ideomotor movements that affect the V-shaped branch.

Ouija boards are another example of how ideomotor movements reveal "secrets." Ouija boards (a combination of the French *oui* and German *ja*, words for *yes*) are operated when one or two people lay their fingers lightly on the heart-shaped sliding slab that then moves around the Ouija board answering questions asked by the players. The board contains a written alphabet, numbers, and the words *yes*, and *no*, and *I don't know*. The answers people get with Ouija boards are, of course, expressions of the unconscious as it spells out hidden or not-so-hidden desires through the hypnotic technique of ideomotor movements.

Another ancient game associated with occultism and employing hypnotic techniques is the planchette, a device for "communicating with the spirits." It is a heart-shaped piece of wood with a pencil attached, mounted on castors. When the hand is placed on the wood, the pencil writes automatically and the words spelled out are believed to be communications from the spirit world. This is once again an example of how the unconscious mind can find expression through ideomotor movements.

Mass Hypnosis

Group dynamics are vastly more difficult to delineate than individual ones. Group psychotherapy, for instance, has never been as well worked out as individual psychological structure. The reactions of one person to an event such as hypnosis are obviously easier to study and understand than the reactions of an entire group. However, a brief glance at the most commonly perceived example of the phenomenon of "mass hypnosis" will show how the elements of hypnosis can be utilized to create an aura of hypersuggestibility in large groups of people. This example is, of course, the massive use of hypnotic techniques in Nazi Germany.

The Nazi propaganda film *Triumph of the Will* provides a vivid record of the induction techniques carefully masterminded by Nazi propaganda minister Dr. Joseph Goebbels. One of the goals of the party meetings was to rally the German population to support the Nazi party and its aims. History proved that Goebbels's efforts were successful.

The stupefying displays of visual and auditory stimuli staged by Goebbels created an atmosphere of extreme group cohesiveness and expectancy. For example, the scenes of torchlight parades, huge amphitheaters filled with people resplendently uniformed, hundreds of searchlights pointing straight up in the sky, massed arrays of bands playing military marches, and goose-stepping, black-uniformed storm troopers were all used in the film *Triumph of the Will* for the express purpose of building mass expectations to a crescendo. When this was accomplished, the people were no longer mere spectators; they became part of the ritual, part of the Nazi phenomenon, and dedicated themselves wholly to the party and its goals.

At the party rallies as well as in his regular public appearances, Hitler and his entourage would make their appearance at the psychologically appropriate moment. Hitler himself usually rode in an open limousine with a countenance of complete command. The mass response to him was overwhelming, and many films of the era show the almost catatonic behavior of the crowds. Men and women would weep and faint, falling to the ground with hands out-stretched to the passing fascist leader as if he were a god incarnate.

When Hitler spoke in public, he employed hypnotic techniques with the cunning of an expert in the art of fanning a crowd to a peak of excitement. He often delayed his appearance, sometimes for as long as two hours, until the feeling in the auditorium was exactly "right." When he finally made his entrance, the audience was putty in his hands, easily manipulated to believe the most outrageous dogma.

Perhaps one reason why so many people associate "mass hypnosis" with Nazi Germany is our unwillingness to believe normal people in normal circumstances capable of committing the crimes that took place in Germany under Hitler's regime. It is more comfortable for us to believe that the German people were under the power of a master hypnotist, to whom they submitted totally. Alas, it is not so simple. We can notice only that hypnoticlike techniques were used, and they probably contributed to the end result.

Hypnosis and Sexuality

There is a strong connection made in the minds of many people between hypnosis and sexuality. This undoubtedly springs from the stereotype of a powerful male hypnotist and his frail female subject, as well as the misconception that hypnosis renders one powerless to resist temptation.

The connection between hypnosis and sexuality is seldom discussed in most formal literature, even though, as previously mentioned, many believe Freud gave up the practice of hypnosis because he found it "too seductive." In my practice, women participants in group sessions sometimes feel compelled to bring along a friend to act as a "chaperone," so uneasy are they with the sexual implications they think inherent in hypnosis.

Just as hypnosis allows us to relinquish some of our more conscious controls and to be aware of our deeper feelings and needs, it often allows us to feel sexual feelings we don't experience under ordinary conditions. Stage hypnotists and charlatans take advantage of the implications of sexuality, using (and abusing) this situation to create a titillating atmosphere for their antics. One of the most common questions asked about hypnosis is, "Can you really get people to take off their clothes on stage if they are under hypnosis?" The answer, of course, is "not unless the person truly wishes to do so." Most people do not.

At a national meeting of a scientific society I attended several years ago, hypnosis was demonstrated for a professional audience using autogenic training techniques. Hypnosis was induced in the audience and, in the course of the demonstration, it was suggested that members would feel a pleasant sensation in their pelvis. I paid close attention to the reactions of the group and noticed that several people spontaneously came out of their trance at this point. Others began to look decidedly uncomfortable. When the demonstration was completed and the audience returned to their normal states, one man raised his hand and said, "This may sound funny, but I don't remember anything you said after 'you will now feel a very pleasant feeling in your chest.'" (This had been the last thing said before the pelvis suggestion.) This man had developed spontaneous amnesia for any statement about feeling pleasure in his pelvis. He was red-faced and obviously uncomfortable, maybe even slightly angry. By accident, later in the day, I saw him at the checkout counter of the hotel. He was angrily and agitatedly demanding to check out because, he said, "My bed is too hard!"

This is a good illustration of how our deeply repressed feelings of sexuality can make us uncomfortable when they are close to the surface of our consciousness. I do not believe that hypnosis per se stirs sexual feelings in people, but I do believe that the sexual feelings we all constantly control, the ones that come from within us, are something brought to a conscious level or nearly so by the changed state of consciousness in hypnosis. This is one of the reasons I recommend that hypnosis not be done on a casual basis, simply for fun, or as party tricks. People should be aware that, under hypnosis, they may feel all kinds of feelings, but that these will remain under their conscious control, if necessary.

Conclusion

Hypnosis is a form of mental discipline, a capacity that lies dormant in most humans but has obviously been utilized for centuries, whether understood or not. Since medical "discovery" of hypnosis in the eighteenth century, public acceptance has waxed and waned through the years, with alternating periods of enthusiasm and prejudice.

Hypnosis has been misunderstood, exploited, and sensationalized even as researchers and clinicians con-

172   THE COMPLETE BOOK OF SELF-HYPNOSIS

tinue to study its dimensions. This stormy course through history proves only that the concepts of hypnosis are controversial and have been used both to enhance and degrade the quality of life. Perhaps by seeing it in the light of an innate essence of self-control, both psychic and physical, humankind can continue to use hypnosis as always while studying and understanding it in a more rational way.

10. Expanding Your Horizons

Now that you have a solid background in the principles of self-hypnosis, techniques, history, and the most common clinical applications to habit changes and health improvements, let us take a look at some other ways hypnosis can be applied to make the inner changes you desire.

This chapter will briefly cover a wide variety of conditions that respond well to hypnotic techniques, and give you more information on gaining mastery of your unconscious needs and motivations. The door, as usual, remains open for you to innovate, using the skills you have already learned and applying them to your own particular condition, your life style, and whatever areas of your life you have decided hypnosis can help.

Once again, it is important to stress that hypnosis per se does not automatically guarantee success, just as enrolling in a dance class won't make you a dancer overnight. It takes practice and dedication to reach any goal. What you get out of your hypnotic experiences will depend on the effort you expend.

Childbirth

Expectant parents today have many choices available to them to help them through pregnancy and childbirth, choices ranging from the latest innovations in prepared childbirth to the more traditional birth methods. Currently, most obstetric practitioners are supportive of parents preparing and participating in the normal delivery of their children. As in all things, a sense of mastery and control over a situation increases the probability of getting through it with ease and good health. In childbirth, this sense of mastery and control is far preferable to submitting passively and fearfully to what other people plan.

The Lamaze method of prepared childbirth is perhaps the most popular technique. The Lamaze breathing techniques give a couple the sense that they can do something to speed and promote the healthy delivery of their child. The laboring mother knows what to expect each step along the way and is therefore not subject to unreasoning fears and panic.

Self-hypnosis can be a most useful adjunct to the Lamaze method or any other prepared childbirth technique. As a matter of fact, the tense-and-relax exercises practiced by Lamaze couples are a form of Jacobsonian relaxation, and employ all the elements of hypnosis: concentration, distraction, and inward focus.

The first and most important step in preparing for childbirth is the decision to bring it under your control. Next, sharing the experience with someone you can trust (your mate, a close friend, your doctor, or anyone else who can be supportive and offer psychological comfort) is also important. And, of course, educating yourself as thoroughly as possible about pregnancy and childbirth increases both your knowledge and your sense of control. Many books, films, and articles are available on this subject. A wealth of information may be gleaned from parents who have successfully produced children. People love to talk about the happy experiences in their lives, and prepared childbirth is almost always a joyous occasion for both parents.

One useful technique to start practicing at least three months prior to the baby's due date is Jacobsonian relaxation, with concentration on relaxing the legs and thighs, noticing how under hypnosis you can control and increase both tension and relaxation in those areas. As you practice tightening and relaxing your legs and thighs (without allowing the sensations to travel into your abdominal area, since you don't wish to bring on the highly unlikely event of premature labor), you will associate this pleasant experience with the contractions of labor.

Another useful technique to practice is going on a search for tension. Under hypnosis, locate any source of body tension and let it flow out of your body through your legs. This can be applied during labor as a way to disperse the feeling of pressure as the uterus contracts. Allow your uncomfortable feelings of pressure to flow out of your body through your legs.

Under self-hypnosis, you can create a sensation of numbness in your hands, a numbness you can then pass into other areas of your body through touching. Practice transferring the numbness in your hands to your abdomen, your thighs, and your perineum (vaginal-rectal area). With practice, you should be able to accomplish this without touching your perineum, since hospital deliveries have strong injunctions about sterile conditions during childbirth.

Active fantasy is another useful technique to use during labor and delivery. Associate the feelings of uterine pressure and contractions with the certainty that those sensations are healthy and natural and are pushing the baby out into the world. Change the fear of pain into a feeling of healthy pressure, knowing your body is working as it should to accomplish the safe delivery of your child.

Time distortion, if practiced regularly before childbirth, can help both parents make the time of labor seem to pass more quickly. Focus and concentrate on the expectation of seeing the baby; look ahead to the thrill of the family union that will take place when the baby is born.

Another technique, used in some primitive tribes, is transference of pain from one person to another. Under hypnosis, the father-to-be might take on some of the sensations of pain and thus share the experience of labor and healthy contractions. This way, the participating father can use hypnosis to avoid feeling helpless, knowing he serves a useful and necessary function and can experience, at least vicariously, the joys of childbirth.

Parenting

Parenting is probably the biggest dilemma in human culture. No one would dream of entrusting a delicate computer to someone with no training in how to operate it, yet human infants are regularly entrusted to rank amateurs for the difficult and demanding job of child-rearing. About the only training we have is our own upbringing. If our parents were lovers and givers, then we have a fairly decent chance to be good parents. But, if we were raised with violence or shame, it will be difficult to raise our own children differently, no matter how much we might want to.

Even the best parents often feel angry and frustrated. One young mother confessed ruefully that she had never been able to understand the crime of child abuse until she had a baby of her own. Then it became horrifyingly clear to her how some people might be unable to cope with the rage and frustration sometimes encountered in parenthood. Often harried parents find themselves striking out at their children, finding their annoyance with their children to be the final straw of a difficult day. They vent the day's accumulated anger on their offspring.

Hypnotic techniques can help you increase your patience and forebearance, letting you handle your frustrations more efficiently. A technique of distancing may be of use in these situations. One patient described a day he was feeding his ten-month-old baby, becoming more and more uptight with the spilled food, the whining of the four-year-old, and the pressure to get the feeding done and the dishes washed. He said, "I just kind of slipped into hypnosis at that point, looked at the situation in a different way, and discovered that what was really important was for the baby to enjoy her meal, the four-year-old to get the attention she needed, and for the three of us to have a good experience together. Getting that last spoonful of carrots in just wasn't a life or death issue."

This kind of report is quite common in my practice. Patients often tell me that the skills learned in self-hypnosis have an invaluable side effect in helping them cope better with the strains of parenthood. "My kids have noticed a difference in me!" they say happily, or, as one mother told me her daughter remarked, "Gee, Mom, you don't yell so much any more!"

Several hypnotic sessions devoted to autoanalysis of your relationship with your children can provide helpful insights into the problems you have as a parent. Search for patterns of bullying, anger, and rage, and try to identify their source. Try putting yourself in your child's place, and see how it would feel to have yourself as a parent. If, in self-analysis, you find yourself locked in a struggle with your children, try to use your intelligence and adult understanding to gain insights into the struggle instead of winning by brute force. Try to harness the power you and your children expend fighting with each other, turning it toward a mutually positive experience for each of you.

Toilet training struggles are a good illustration of this technique. Many parents see the final putting away of diapers as a day of liberation for themselves, and they experience great frustrations when their child resists cooperating in that goal. Using self-hypnosis can help you realize that your child has control over his or her bladder and bowel function, and the struggle you are locked into is over the child's autonomy. Try to find a way to turn bowel and urinary functions over to the child, so that he or she may feel good about whatever she or he decides to do about it. If the decision is to continue wetting, let the child feel good about it, saying, "Okay, it's your pants, your urine, your choice." Often the true and honest relinquishing of the struggle for control will allow the child to solve the question in a positive way, to enjoy being dry because he or she chooses it.

Whatever patterns of struggle you find in your autoanalytic sessions, use hypnosis to identify them clearly. Then try to discover a way to turn the power of that struggle with your children into a more positive avenue. Of course, you must still control your children, but you can learn to exercise that control while allowing your children to feel good about themselves and their relationship with you.

While hypnotic skills can be used efficiently to solve specific child-rearing problems, its biggest benefit is perhaps more general. In learning to relax and concentrate, and allowing those feelings to linger on after self-hypnotic sessions, most parents report an easing of family pressure and an improved atmosphere of patience, calmness, and love.

Insomnia

Almost everyone is familiar with the awful feeling of lying in bed wide awake, knowing they will have to stumble through the next day feeling tired and drained. The fear of not getting enough sleep can feed on itself, making you more tense the harder you concentrate on your predicament.

Hypnosis can be a powerful inducement to sleep and is, in fact, often used by people who have no idea that they are employing hypnotic techniques. Counting sheep, a time-honored cliché, is simply guided imagery, the rhythmic counting of fluffy white sheep as they glide over a meadow fence.

If you are troubled by insomnia, you can set up a hypnotic situation before you go to bed, and then use self-hypnosis to fall into a deep and healthy sleep. Decide on a time you feel is best for you to go to bed, and then use the hour before that time to do whatever is most relaxing for you. You may want to induce hypnosis and use direct suggestion to tell yourself that you will feel sleepy at your appointed bedtime; you will feel your eyes grow heavy then and fall into a deep and satisfying slumber. When you do go to bed, use progressive muscular relaxation or concentration on a physiological act, such as respiration, to induce hypnosis easily and most relaxingly. Tell yourself that as you relax you will drift comfortably into a normal, healthy sleep and awake refreshed in the morning.

Many people enjoy the technique of active fantasy to induce sleep. They often decide to take an imaginary trip, choosing a location they would like to visit leisurely. It might be Minneapolis or Marrakesh—the destination is not important because you don't plan to arrive. Use self-hypnosis to enjoy the journey, taking lots of stops along the way to appreciate the scenery, allowing yourself to travel slowly, savoring every detail of the roadway and noticing how relaxing it is to meander along in no particular hurry. Feel yourself grow increasingly sleepy until you finally curl up under a hedge or in a haystack sound asleep.

Dental Hypnosis

You are born with the buds of all the teeth you will ever have, so it is important to take good care of them. Regular dental checkups are necessary for oral hygiene, and many dentists use hypnosis in place of or as an adjunct to anesthesia when necessary to deaden pain. You can probably find a dentist in your area who practices hypnosis, if that appeals to you.

You can also use self-hypnosis in place of Novocain on your own, making sure to practice numbing your mouth before you visit the dentist. To do this, induce hypnosis by your usual method and then practice recreating the feeling of numbness in your mouth that you have experienced before under Novocain. All the information is stored in the computer that is your brain. All you have to do is play back the tapes to relive that sensation of numbness in your mouth. Notice how you can achieve oral numbness on your own. Another method, already discussed, is to use hypnosis to numb your hand and then transfer the sensation to your mouth by touching.

For some people, much of the agony of dental procedures is the anticipation of pain. One woman I know insists on Novocain for simply cleaning her teeth, so tense and frightened is she when she enters the dentist's office. After learning self-hypnosis, she told me that she applied it on her regular dental visit and became so relaxed that she actually fell asleep in the examining chair.

One useful way to use self-hypnosis in preparation for dental procedures is to set up a hierarchy of anticipations, dealing with them one by one under hypnosis until they lose their aura of fear and pain. Induce hypnosis and imagine yourself calling for an appointment (this is sometimes the most difficult task for those who dread dental appointments). Go over your expectations of what that will be like until you feel confident enough to make the call. Continue your hierarchy of anticipation by imagining yourself on the morning of your appointment, driving to the dentist's office, sitting in the waiting room, getting into the chair. Under hypnosis, see yourself with the suction instrument in your mouth. Look over the equipment, feel the dentist touch your teeth, noticing that it is just a sensation, not pain. Then allow yourself to hear the drill; relax and feel the sense of vibration in your mouth, steady vibrations that are not pain. Thinking ahead to a dreaded experience relieves the anxiety and tension, and familiarizing yourself with the procedure will help you relax. Go through this hierarchy of anticipation as often as necessary until it is no longer uncomfortable for you.

Another technique is posthypnotic suggestion. At home, induce hypnosis as deeply as possible and tell yourself that once you sit in the dentist's chair you will go far away to a pleasant place and remain there until you hear the dentist say, "That is all for today. You can get up now." (Be sure to explain what you are doing ahead of time to the dentist.)

These techniques can be useful for other types of medical appointments that are uncomfortable for you. Many women use hypnotic relaxation for gynecological visits, and hypnosis can ease the discomfort of examinations as well as injections and blood donations. Relaxation is the key to ridding yourself of this type of anxiety.

Nervous Habits

Most of us have some kind of nervous habit that we do more or less unconsciously, such as nail biting, teeth grinding, gulping, hair twisting, lip biting, knuckle cracking, or ear pulling. Nervous habits can be unhealthy as well as unattractive. Self-hypnosis can help you break the habit, if that is what you wish to do.

In my practice, nervous habits are usually a secondary symptom, not the primary complaint of the patients I see. Nervous habits are usually of long duration, and they are often adult replacements of childhood security symbols, such as thumbsucking or blanket fondling. As adults, we would feel foolish sucking our thumbs, but biting our nails or twisting our hair is somehow more acceptable to our subconscious need for security in tension-filled lives.

If you consciously want to discard a nervous habit, perhaps the first step would be using self-hypnosis to check out that decision through ideomotor movements. Using the technique described in chapter 5, ask yourself if you are ready to give up your habit.

One way to ease out of an unwanted habit is to set up a stimulus-response situation under hypnosis. When you have induced self-hypnosis, re-create the stimulus that results in the habit you wish to change. Let's take the problem of knuckle cracking. When you feel the urge to crack your knuckles, hook up that stimulus with a different response. You may glance briefly at your hands, take a deep breath, and experience instant relaxation. Practice this technique until the new stimulus-response pattern is automatic.

Another technique is substitution. Substitute another, more acceptable and less damaging action for the habit you wish to change. Every time you feel like grinding your teeth, for instance, clench your fist instead. Use hypnosis to reinforce this decision, perhaps by direct suggestion.

Nervous habits respond well to aversion techniques. Under self-hypnosis, associate the pleasure you derive from your habit with something unpleasant or disgusting. Picture your fingernails as tin foil, for example, and experience how unsettling it would be to bite into tin foil with your teeth. Or picture your knuckles as delicate glass ornaments that, when cracked, would shatter. Make up your own aversion techniques that are particularly distasteful to you.

If your nervous habit is in reality a reflection of underlying tensions that would be best dealt with in therapy, then you should seek consultation with a psychiatrist or psychologist. If removing a deeply important source of tension relief leaves you feeling lost and depressed, then find a competent professional and get the help you need.

Mild Phobias

Phobias are often best understood as displacement of an internalized prohibition that is unacceptable to the conscious mind. The phobia offers a substitution, a means of remaining unaware of the unacceptable feeling or impulse. For instance, the child whose angry impulses at a sibling are strong and frightening might be unable to face or deal with the desire to hurt the sibling, and so find expression as a fear of other children. I once treated a family who allowed no overt show of anger at any time. Although there were violent and angry feelings within the family, they were ignored and repressed. Everyone in the family had a fear of sharp objects, and the grandfather periodically dulled all the knives in the house and broke the points off scissors. This is an example of a severe phobia that is best dealt with in therapy.

Any strong and unreasonable fear that interferes with your ability to function or that limits your life style should lead you to seek professional counselling. Help is possible through therapy or desensitization, a technique similar to the self-help methods we will discuss, but which is closely followed and monitored by a psychiatrist or psychologist.

Mild phobias are those fears that are unreasonable and limiting but do not seriously hamper normal living. Some mild phobias that can be helped with self-hypnosis include mild fear of crowds, fear of flying, fear of elevators, fear of heights, and so on.

Obviously, a phobia can be a sign of psychological conflict that can't be expressed in any other way and is particularly resistant to exposure by self-analysis. Still, the first step in conquering any unreasonable fear is to attempt to find out exactly what it is you fear. Self-analysis under self-hypnosis may provide an answer, but, even if it doesn't, you can go on to use other hypnotic techniques to put your phobia behind you.

You may want to build up a hierarchy of fears, using self-hypnosis to gradually accustom yourself to whatever is causing your phobic reaction. If it is fear of elevators, for instance, you might start by imagining yourself standing outside a building you know has an elevator. Then, see yourself going inside and standing in front of the elevator. Next, push the button and experience what it means to wait for the elevator to arrive, listening to the whir of the motor and the sound of the pulleys. When you have familiarized yourself with all of those feelings while remaining relaxed under self-hypnosis, imagine yourself stepping into the elevator, looking at the panel of buttons, and watching the doors close. Push the button for the floor you want, and concentrate on relaxing, noticing how the lights come on at each floor and associating that event with deep relaxation. Finally, see yourself in the elevator as it arrives at your floor. Step off, congratulating yourself for having accomplished what you feared to do. Practice this technique until the fear is lessened and you can approach an elevator in a relaxed frame of mind.

Posthypnotic suggestions are useful when you have reached the point where you feel ready to try out your now nonphobic reactions. If you have a fear of crowds, for instance, give yourself a posthypnotic suggestion that the comfort of being with other people will replace the fear of crowds.

Substitution is another useful hypnotic technique for conquering unreasonable fears. If you have a mild phobic reaction to airplane flights, use hypnosis to prepare for your next air journey. Under hypnosis, remind yourself that while you can't control the plane, you can control your feelings, and then substitute something relaxing for the fear. If you enjoy reading, for instance, pick out a book or magazine you have been wanting to read and use self-hypnosis to concentrate on substituting the pleasure and relaxation of reading for the fear of flying. Use hypnosis to look forward to the experience of flying because it offers the chance to relax.

Salesmanship and Stage Fright

Public speaking is a particularly worrisome fear for many people. Anxiety about self-assertion refers back to early insecurities, and understanding this often helps dispel the fear. Salespeople, performers, politicians, teachers, and religious leaders, to name only a few, are all in professions that require them to speak with confidence and assurance in order to sell their product. Unfortunately, this is often difficult for many people.

A colleague of mine told me about the time he was called suddenly to give a presentation to the president of his company. He had only a short while to prepare his remarks, and he was very nervous. He walked over to the president's office with a friend, who noticed his tense behavior. In the few minutes it took to walk to that office, this colleague realized that his tension was probably going to interfere with his ability to make the presentation in the best possible light. So, he used self-hypnosis rapidly to relax, astonishing his friend, who asked, "What did you do? You were wound up tighter than a drum and now you are back on an even keel." Using self-hypnosis to relax helped this colleague make a confident presentation, and even the president of his company remarked on the ease and familiarity with which he presented his work.

Using self-hypnosis to relax before a speaking engagement can give you the self-confidence to speak with sureness and authority. You can also use it to dispel fear of the audience by choosing to see them as people who are hanging on your every word, people who are eager to hear what you have to say.

Use the tension of public encounters to work for you instead of against you, a chance to show what you know in your own unique way. Under self-hypnosis, remind yourself that you don't know everything, but that is perfectly okay. Build up a series of personal catchwords to increase your self-esteem. When that has been accomplished, it will be evident to your clients or audience.

When I feel tension building up before a public speaking engagement, I use self-hypnosis to turn that tension into enjoyment of a chance to do well at my job. I remind myself that it isn't all up to me. The audience has the option to take what I teach or not. Relaxing under self-hypnosis helps me slow down and keep my thoughts clear.

Memory, Studying, and Test Taking

Self-hypnosis can increase your level of awareness and concentration, making you more alert without being tense. Just as a salesperson can see a sales meeting as a chance to show what he or she knows, the student can see a test as the same chance.

The long hours of studying in medical school results in backaches, fatigue, and dulled thinking for many medical students, including me. To ease those tensions and clear my mind, I used self-hypnosis to smooth over the distractions and increase my level of awareness. The key to improved memory, studying, and test taking is relaxation, concentration, and distractibility, three very important hypnotic elements.

To improve your memory, use self-hypnosis to relax and think of the fact you need to remember. Then, close your eyes and see what personally significant association comes to mind. When the fact you wish to memorize is associated with something meaningful to you, it will become as readily available to you as, for instance, your own birth date.

A quick way to use self-hypnosis to remember the name of someone you ought to know but whose name you have temporarily forgotten is this: Use a quick hypnotic relaxation technique to clear your mind, making it smooth and tension free, an empty movie screen upon which you can project the face of the person whose name you are searching for. Relax and allow that name to spring to mind, like actor's credits on the silver screen.

When fatigue and boredom interfere with your ability to study, self-hypnosis can come to the rescue. Close your eyes and relax, inducing trance quickly. Then allow yourself a mental shot of adrenalin, recapitulating past feelings of excitement, energy, and vigor. You have all the memories of those emotions stored in your brain, and you can reexperience them under self-hypnosis. Clear away the fatigue and cobwebs in your brain, and return to studying refreshed and eager to face the challenge.

Autogenic training is often helpful before taking a test. Go off by yourself and use self-hypnosis to relax. Then give yourself commands, such as, "My forehead is cool, my mind is clear and relaxed. I can remember all that I need to know. I will take the test calmly, reading the instructions carefully, without any need to rush." In this frame of mind, test taking loses much of its tension and fear, becoming instead a chance for the student to shine.

Getting High

Some people describe the experience of hypnosis as similar to, though not exactly like, "getting high." Your expectations about what hypnosis will be like play a large part in determining the experience for you. People who enjoy the feeling of euphoria commonly associated with getting high find self-hypnosis an easy, healthy way to experience those sensations.

Each person is the director of his or her experiences under hypnosis. Altering your state of consciousness by this method is preferred by many to taking drugs or alcohol. Self-hypnosis is healthy and free, a way to get high without suffering a hangover the next morning or losing one's sense of safety and caution for the amount of time the alcohol or drug is active in the bloodstream.

A few patients who have used self-hypnosis for this purpose reported the actual physical symptoms of getting high. They giggled a lot, felt their eyes grow heavy, and relaxed to the point of looseness.

To get high on self-hypnosis, simply induce trance for no particular reason other than to feel good. You might want to re-create your last exuberant experience, a time when you felt wonderful. Allow yourself to smile and let that experience happen again in your mind. Remind yourself that you can re-create these feelings whenever it is useful, whenever you want to have a good time.

Self-hypnosis offers feelings of euphoria with none of the drawbacks, no hangover, no possibility of a criminal record, no concern about being able to drive home safely, no waking up the next morning with an impaired memory. You can enjoy the same good time without abusing your body with alcohol or drugs.

Case Studies

Case One

Mrs. X., a native of Thailand, was the mother of a newborn girl. Her obstetrician called me to ask if I could help. The nurse told me that Mrs. X. was refusing to see her baby and seemed deeply depressed. The staff had tried everything they could think of to initiate the mother-child bonding they knew was so important, but nothing had worked so far.

First, I talked to Mrs. X.'s physician, who told me that her patient was upset because Mr. X. had wanted a son. The new mother felt disgraced and sad because she had failed to meet her husband's expectations. The child was the result of an unplanned pregnancy, and there were additional problems in the marriage. Mrs. X., lonely and friendless in a foreign country, had hoped the birth of a son would cement her faltering marriage. "The more we pushed her to see the baby," the nurse explained when I arrived on the ward, "the more she hid her head in her hands and cried. She won't talk to anyone, not even her minister."

When I went to Mrs. X.'s room, I saw a woman of twenty-seven in a clean but unbuttoned gown, her hair slightly unkempt, and a far away look in her eyes. She seemed to be in a daze, as if she were waiting for something.

I introduced myself and began by asking her some medical questions, but she shook her head, indicating she didn't want to talk. Using her apparent negativism and the energy of her withdrawal from the outside world and from her baby, I began to talk in a low, modulated tone. "You don't have to listen to me," I said. "Perhaps you don't want to. You may choose to hear my voice or not. Although I don't understand exactly what you are going through, I do understand that you are feeling lonely."

In a rambling monologue, I went on to talk about how tough it must be to have a shaky marriage in a foreign country with no friends to talk to. I sympathized with her situation and outlined her choices about her baby. She continued to stare at her hands in her lap (eye fixation), and soon I could tell she was in a light to medium hypnotic trance.

"You don't have to feed your baby," I continued. "You don't have to diaper her or rock her or powder her skin. The ward personnel can take care of all that." By this time her eyes were closed and her breathing was deep and regular.

Using words and images I knew would have particular significance for a parent, I concentrated on describing the baby's anatomy. "You don't have to look at your baby," I assured her. "You don't have to examine her tiny hands, her little fingers, her hair. You don't have to look at her feet to see if she has ten toes or how her legs are shaped. Of course, you might be curious and wonder what your baby looks like, but you don't have to pay any attention to her if you don't want to.'' Always I came back to the point that she didn't have to take responsibility for her daughter if she didn't want to.

After fifteen minutes of this, I mentioned that she might begin to notice how the sun was streaming in the window, and it was turning out to be a nice day after all. This brought her gradually out of her trance and she began to cry. We talked for a while about her sadness and how it was okay for her to experience that feeling while she was getting over being sad. When I left, she still seemed confused but was more alert.

Later in the day, the nurse called me to say that Mrs. X. had asked for her baby right after I left and had spent the next forty-five minutes minutely examining the child, undressing it and looking carefully at each section of its anatomy. The nurse was frankly amazed at Mrs. X.'s swift turnabout, but, through indirect hypnotic suggestion, I had simply helped the new mother reconnect her natural curiosity and love for her infant with her conscious mind. Once the bonding was complete, Mrs. X. could focus on her other problems while giving her daughter the attention she needed.

Case Two

Mr. D., a mail carrier in his mid-thirties, came to me for help with a mild phobia that was causing him increasing distress.

"It's dogs," he told me. "I have always been terrified of them, ever since I was a child. I was badly bitten by a stray when I was three years old and had to spend a few days in the hospital. I don't remember much about it, but my mother claims the experience turned her hair gray overnight. She got rid of the puppy we had at the time, and I don't think I have ever touched a dog since then.''

''What has happened recently to make you want to conquer your phobia now?'' I asked.

''Well, it is my son. He is seven now and I have noticed lately that he is as frightened of dogs as I am. I don't want him to go through the same ordeal, and I can't help him much when I am scared to death of dogs myself. I can't even stand to see a dog food commercial on TV. It is that bad.''

I explained how learning self-hypnosis can help many people overcome their phobias, and he expressed interest in trying. Baseball, he told me, was his favorite form of relaxation, and he enjoyed going to baseball games and watching them on television. We induced hypnosis by active fantasy—he concentrated on seeing himself in his most comfortable chair, watching a game on TV, and letting a feeling of relaxation sweep over him.

At our next session, he reported that daily practice had shown results, and he was enjoying the experience. ''But I don't see how this is going to help me with dogs,'' he added. We induced hypnosis using the same technique and concentrating on baseball imagery. Then I asked him to imagine a little dog running out on the field during the game and see how the umpire and players had to stop the game to get the dog off the field so it wouldn't be hurt. I asked him to see the people chasing the little dog and imagine how the dog would lick them and bark happily at being included in the game.

The principle here, of course, was that Mr. D. couldn't be afraid and relaxed at the same time. Introducing a friendly, nonthreatening little animal into his pleasant baseball imagery gave him a way to desensitize his fear.

From now on, I suggested, he might want to think of baseball every time he saw a dog, to keep uppermost in his thoughts the image of the playful harmless creature who had interrupted the game. Thinking of baseball in this way would induce relaxation and erode the phobia. With practice, he would learn to associate what he feared, dogs, with what relaxed him most, baseball. By turning his mild phobia into a simple respect for a possibly dangerous dog, he was able to break the spell of his own fears and avoid passing them on to his son.

Case Three

Ms. C., a nineteen-year-old college student, had been suffering hyperhydrosis since the age of four. Hyperhydrosis, a condition which causes the hands to sweat profusely, made it necessary for Ms. C. to carry towels with her wherever she went to soak up the moisture. When she held her hands downward, water actually dripped off them onto the floor. She was referred to me by a dermatologist who was considering surgery (nerve cutting) since none of the medication she was on seemed to help at all.

Ms. C., an attractive, active woman, was working

her way through college by managing a small restaurant. She had learned to live with her condition, giving up hobbies she enjoyed, such as sewing, because her wet hands soaked the material and made working on it impossible. Instead, she had taken up pottery, a craft which made good use of wet hands.

At the time I met her, I was chief resident at a large teaching hospital and was working under another psychiatrist, Dr. H. He explained the fundamentals of hypnosis to Ms. C. and told her that he thought the skill of self-hypnosis might eventually help her control her hyperhydrosis. She was anxious to try.

Dr. H. first induced hypnosis by eye fixation and Ms. C. appeared to go into a light trance, although she reported that she didn't feel she had been hypnotized. Next, we used Jacobsonian relaxation, which she described as enjoyable, but once again reported only the mildest sense of hypnosis. During this procedure, Dr. H. and I noticed that she was leaning toward the left, toward the chair where I was sitting. Spontaneously, she told us that the left side of her body had reacted differently under hypnosis in a way that she described as "a flowing toward the left." In fact, her left eye got red and tearful while her right eye did not. From this, we knew that her natural reaction was the defense of psychological splitting, dividing things in half: good and bad, work and play, etc. Having two therapists in the room augmented this splitting technique, and we tried to take advantage of that to help her learn to help herself.

We instructed her to practice these hypnotic techniques at home and made an appointment for the following week. Our plan was to have her learn to move the sweating into her right hand entirely and then into her feet, where it would be less obvious and she could cope with it by simply changing her socks, a definite improvement over carrying towels.

To our surprise, when she returned she told us she had begun to control the sweating on her own, having noticed that her left hand was much drier when she practiced relaxing under self-hypnosis. We congratulated her and suggested she might want to try using visual imagery as an induction method, perhaps concentrating on her collection of tapestries, which she had told us decorated the walls of her room.

Two weeks later, at our third session, Ms. C. reported more progress. "I can cut it off in both hands now," she said, "when I really concentrate. But sometimes, at work, if I am really busy it comes back." We suggested that time and more practice would help that and she readily agreed. "I noticed something strange," she told us as she was leaving. "I was sitting on the rug at home, staring at a tapestry and feeling really good, very relaxed, and confident. Then I became aware of a sensation building throughout my whole body, a feeling of warmth and oneness with the world. The sun was shining in through the window and lighting up the tapestry, and I just felt incredibly high! It was a calm, glowing feeling that stayed with me the rest of the day."

A month later she called to report that she had developed a technique she could use at work. She called it "blanking out" and induced hypnosis swiftly by pressing her hands together whenever she felt tensions mount, a situation that in the past had made her hands sweat more. As soon as she pressed her hands together, she said, she felt the same sense of calmness and relaxation she had learned through self-hypnosis. "I am handling people and stress much better now," she said, laughing.

Epilogue

In this book we have seen many examples of how hypnotic techniques and self-hypnosis can work, sometimes dramatically and sometimes in a more subtle and gradual way. We encourage you to use these techniques in a serious fashion, always keeping in mind that the ultimate objectives are increased sense of well-being, increased responsibility for your own health, and even possibly a deeper understanding and control of your potential best friend, yourself. We hope that you can learn to let your body and your feelings work for you instead of against you, and wish you the best of luck in the endeavor.

Index

Active fantasy, 34–35, 79; in childbirth, 176; for insomnia, 180–81
Age regression, 58–59
American Medical Association, 163
American Psychological Association, 163
Amnesia, 6
Anger, 61–62; and overeating, 69; and parenthood, 177, 178; and personality, 55; and smoking, 89
Anxiety, 8, 49, 74
Autoanalysis, 48–65; beginning, 56–57; discarding personality patterns in, 62–64; for pain control 122–27; and sex life, 141–42; and smoking, 92–102; and weight control, 70–77
Autogenic training, 39
Aversion techniques, 75–76

Back pain, 135–39
Bernheim, Hippolyte, 162
Bible, the, 157
Blood pressure, 5, 7, 105–7
Body feelings, 3–4

Body image, 71–73, 141
Body part, focusing on, 31–32, 148–49
Braid, James, 160
Breathing techniques, 32–34
Breuer, Josef, 162
British Medical Association, 163

Cancer: pain and, 115; and smoking, 91–92
Charcot, Jean-Martin, 12, 161
Childbirth, 174–77
Children: parenting, 177–79; and self-hypnosis, 9
Chronic obstructive pulmonary disease, 90
Chronic pain. See Pain control
Cigarettes, 85–112. See also Smoking
"Click," 37, 44–45
Compromise Formation, 50, 52
Concentration, 5–6, 8

Dentistry, and hypnosis, 181–83
Depression: and personality, 54–55; and self-hypnosis, 8–9

Diet, 73–77. *See also*
  Weight control
Distractibility, 8
Divorce: and group
  hypnosis, 45; and self-
  hypnosis 9–10
Dream interpretation, 60–61
Drugs, and self-hypnosis,
  10

Ego structure, 50
Emotional problems: and
  obesity, 68; and self-
  analysis, 49; and self-
  hypnosis, 8–10
Emphysema, 86
Esdaile, James, 160–61
Eyes, 5; fixation of, 30–31

Fantasy. *See* Active fantasy
Fingers, 22–26, 31–32
Focal point, 20–21
Food, 67–69. *See also* Diet;
  Obesity; Weight control
Freud, Sigmund, 53, 140,
  162–63

Gag reflex, 6
Gastrointestinal symptoms, 6
Goebbels, Joseph, 168
Group hypnosis, 45–46. *See
  also* Mass hypnosis
Guided imagery (in weight
  control), 77

Hallucinations, 6
Hands, 22–26, 31–32;
  clasping, 36; levitation of,
  42–43
Headaches, 115
Health problems, 113–39;
  and smoking, 89–92. *See
  also* Emphysema;
  Hypertension; Weight
  control
Heartbeat, 5, 33

Hierarchy of fears, 97; and
  phobias, 186
Hitler, Adolf, 168
Hunger, controlling, 74–76
Hyperhydrosis, 196–97
Hypertension, 105–7
Hypnosis: American Medical
  Association on, 163;
  American Psychological
  Association on, 163; in
  Bible, 157; body feelings
  in, 3–4; definition of, 1;
  dental, 181–83; as
  entertainment, 164–65;
  group, 45–47, 167–69;
  history of, 154–72;
  induced v. self-, 13–15;
  myths of, 11–13; and
  sexuality, 169–72;
  techniques for, 29–47;
  visual imagery in, 3–4.
  See also Posthypnotic
  suggestion; Self-hypnosis;
  Trance
Hypnotic subject, traits of,
  7–8
Hypnotic techniques, 29–47
Hypnotic trance. *See* Trance
Hysterical personality, 53–
  54

Ideomotor movements, 70–
  71, 81, 94; and occult,
  166, 167
Impotence, 147–50
Indians, American, 157–58
Induced hypnosis, 13–15
Inner-centeredness, 6
Insomnia, 180–81
Instantaneous gratification,
  89
Intelligence, 7
Intimacy, 140, 152
"Inward focus," 4

Jewelry, 21

Karate, 158
Key word, 43–45
Kinesthetic feelings, 3–4

Lamaze method of
   childbirth, 174–75
Liebeault, A., 161
Loss, replacing, 96–97
Love, 140
Lungs, 96. *See also*
   Breathing techniques

Mass hypnosis, 167–69
Medical problems. *See* Pain
   control
Medicine, organized, 163–
   64
Memory improvement, 189–
   90
Mesmer, Anton, 155, 158–
   60
Migraine, 115
Mini-relaxation, 98
Motivation, 8
Mourning, and hypnosis, 9,
   45
Muscles: control of, 36;
   progressive relaxation of,
   37–38

Nancy School (France), 162
Negative conditioning, 76,
   100–1
Nervous habits, 183–85
"Neuro-hypnosis," 160

Obesity, 66–84; case studies
   of, 78–84; endogenous,
   66, 67; exogenous, 66;
   hypnotic techniques for,
   73–77
Obsessive personality, 52–
   53
Occult, 165–67
Oral gratification, 88
Orgasm, achieving, 142–47

Pain: anticipation of, 114–
   15; biology of, 119–21;
   definition of, 113–14;
   emotions and, 118–19. *See
   also* Pain control
Pain control, 113–39; case
   histories of, 127–39; and
   dentistry, 181–83; self-
   hypnosis for, 122–27
Panic control, 96–97
Parenting, 177–79
Pendulum method, 40–
   41
Personality, 49–55;
   definition of, 51; and
   hypnosis, 7–8; patterns
   of, 61–64; traits, 52–
   55
Phobias, 185–87; case study
   of, 194–96
Posthypnotic suggestion: and
   dentistry, 183; and
   smoking, 101–2; and
   weight control, 76–77
Psychoses: and group
   hypnosis, 45; and self-
   hypnosis, 9
Public speaking, 187–90
Pulse, 32–33
Puysegur, Armand, Marquis
   de, 160

Rapid eye movement, 5
Relaxation, 23, 26, 27; in
   autoanalysis, 56;
   Jacobsonian, 174–75;
   mini-, 98; progressive
   muscular, 37–38
Repression, 50
Respiration, 5
Reticular activating system
   (RAS), 30

Salesmanship, 187–89
Séances, 159
Self-analysis, 48–65

Self-hypnosis, 29–47; body-set for, 20; for childbirth, 174–77; contraindications for, 8–10; environment and, 19–20; as "high," 191–92; and insomnia, 180–81; motives for, 2–3; for pain control, 122–27; personality traits and, 7–8; place for, 19; for public speaking, 187–89; seven steps to, 16–28; and sex life, 140–42; and smoking, 92–102; techniques for, 29–47; and weight control, 70–77. *See also* Autoanalysis; Hypnosis; Posthypnotic suggestion; Trance
Self-produced training, 39
Sex life, 140–53; attractiveness and 69–70; case studies of, 142–53; impotence and, 147–50; and orgasm, 142–47; self-hypnosis and, 141–42
Sleep: v. hypnosis, 12–13; inducing, 180–81
Smoking, 85–112; and cancer, 91–92; case histories of, 102–12; direct suggestions for, 101–2; and health, 89–92; and self-hypnosis, 92–102; techniques to stop, 96–102
Spokesperson (in group hypnosis), 45–46
Stage fright, 187–89

Studying, 189–90
Subconscious thinking, 4
Substitution rewards, 99–100
Surgery, 160–61; in deep trance, 7; in medium trance, 6

Tape recording, 17
Tense and relax, 37–38
Test-taking, 189–90
Thinking experiences, 4
Tobacco. *See* Smoking
Toilet training, 179
Totem, technique, 41–42
Trance, 3–7; and age regression, 58–59; amnesia in, 6; deep, 7; light, 5; medium, 5–6; types of, 4–7; and weight control, 71–73, 74

Unconscious, the, 49

Visual imagery, 4

Weakness, 61, 64
Weight control, 66–84; body image and, 71–72; case studies of, 78–84; diet, 73–77; physician and, 73; reward for, 75; self-analysis and, 70–77; techniques for, 73–77

Yoga, 33, 39

Zen Buddhism, 7

About the Authors

John M. Yates earned his M.D. degree at the University of Oklahoma College of Medicine. He completed a rotating medical internship at Brooke Army Medical Center at San Antonio and finished his psychiatry residency at Letterman Army Medical Center in San Francisco. He was then chief of the Mental Health Clinic at the U.S. Military Academy at West Point, New York. While at West Point, he served as the Brigade Surgeon to the Corps of Cadets.

Dr. Yates is currently in private psychiatric practice in Oklahoma.

Elizabeth S. Wallace has published newspaper and magazine articles, romantic novels and has written for TV.